KINDERGARTEN
IS TOO LATE!

Masaru Ibuka

SIMON AND SCHUSTER: New York

Published by Simon and Schuster
A Division of Gulf & Western Corporation
Simon & Schuster Building
Rockefeller Center
1230 Avenue of the Americas
New York, New York 10020

Manufactured in the United States of America
1 2 3 4 5 6 7 8 9 10

Library of Congress Cataloging in Publication Data

Ibuka, Masaru, date.
  Kindergarten is too late!

    Translation of Yóchien de wa ososugiru.
    1. Education, Preschool. 2. Child development.
I. Title.
LB1140.2.I2913   1977   372.21   78-112

ISBN 0-0671-24036-6

First published in Great Britain by Souvenir Press, Ltd.

CONTENTS

Foreword by GLENN DOMAN   7
Introduction   13

Part I   Infant Potentiality   17
              The Important Period   19
              What a Small Child Can Do   28

**Part II   The Impact of Early
              Experience**   45

**Part III   What Is Good for Young
              Children?**   65

Part IV   Principles of Training   99
              Stimulation and a Sense of Order 101
              Forming Character in Early Life 122
              Creativity and Skills   136

**Part V   Some Things to Avoid and
              a Glance at the Future**   159

KINDERGARTEN IS TOO LATE!

Foreword

by Glenn Doman
Author of *How to Teach Your Baby to Read*

If the gentleness and grace with which this book is written do not conceal the magnificence of what it sets forth, it could, in company with a few other such gentle books, bring about the most glorious and the most gentle of all the revolutions in the history of this world. It is a consummation devoutly to be wished.

Imagine, if you will, a revolution to bring about the most splendid of changes, but a revolution in which there is no bloodshed, no torture, no pain, no freezing feet, no hatred, no starvation, no death, no destruction.

In this gentlest of revolutions there are only two enemies. The first is ancient myths, and the second is the status quo. It is not necessary that ancient traditions be shattered, but only that ancient falsehoods wither away unmourned. It is not necessary that what is presently good be burned to the ground, but only that so much in the world that is presently terrible rust slowly away through disuse.

What Mr. Ibuka's vision could bring about is the destruction of such things as ignorance, illiteracy, insecurity, and uselessness—and who is to say whether that in turn might not reduce poverty, hatred, and killing?

Mr. Ibuka's book makes no such promise, but to the perceptive reader such dreams continually dance across the screen of his mind's eye as he moves from look to thought to image to dream.

What would it take to bring about such wonderful changes? The fall of governments? The destruction of institutions? The burning down of school systems?

Mr. Ibuka makes no such threats, nor has he made us any such golden promises as I have proposed. It is only that I cannot read Mr. Ibuka's book without ending up with such dreams.

Mr. Ibuka's marvelous and gentle book makes no earth-shaking pronouncements of any sort. He simply proposes that tiny children have within them the capacity to learn virtually anything while they are tiny. He proposes that what they learn without any conscious effort at two, three, or four years of age can be learned only with great effort, or may not be learned at all, in later life. He proposes that what adults learn painfully children learn joyfully. He proposes that what adults learn at a snail's pace, tiny children learn almost speedily. He proposes that adults sometimes avoid learning, while tiny children would rather learn than eat.

He states all this in the most charming of manners. His book is simple, straightforward, and crystal clear, and as a result it has about it on every page the ring of truth.

He proposes that among the most difficult tasks man sets himself are such endeavors as learning to read, learning foreign languages, and learning to play the violin or piano. I am a good example of this point. Although I dabble in a dozen foreign languages, as a result of my life work of studying children on every continent and in all settings from the most sophisticated of societies to the most basic of all cultures, I can deal effectively only in my mother tongue. While I enjoy music, I cannot play a musical instrument, nor can I so much as carry a tune properly. While these things are mastered with difficulty by adults, they can be mastered almost without conscious effort by tiny children.

All these things tiny children can master, and they do so easily and joyfully. All that is required for tiny children to grow up speaking many tongues fluently, reading the most complex of languages, doing instant mathematics, swimming, riding horseback, painting in oils, playing the violin, and doing them all with skill is that we give our children love (we commonly do), respect (we rarely do), and joyful exposure to the things we wish them to know.

Is it difficult to imagine that the world would be a richer, saner, safer, lovelier place if all children had mastered languages, arts, and basic sciences before they had grown to be teen-agers, and could then use their teen years to study semantics, philosophy, ethics, and comparative religion as well as advanced arts and advanced science or whatever else they'd like to learn?

Is it difficult to imagine what the world would be like if tiny children had their burning rage to learn fed and fanned instead of smothered with toys and games?

Is it difficult to imagine that the world would be a lovelier place if a three-year-old's hunger to see all there is to see were fed with Michelangelo, Winslow Homer, Manet, Rembrandt, Renoir, Leonardo, and Rockwell, as well as Mickey Mouse and Happy the Clown? For in truth, the tiny child has an infinite appetite to learn all that he does not know, and he has not the slightest shred of judgment as to what is good and what is bad.

Can one doubt that the world would be a saner place if a two-year-old's hunger to hear all that there is to hear were fed with Bach as well as rock, with Beethoven as well as "Mary Had a Little Lamb," with the Sermon on the Mount or the Declaration of Independence as well as Red Riding Hood? For in truth, the tiny child can learn one as easily as the other.

Can one doubt that the world would be a safer place if a three-year-old's hunger to speak were fed with Portuguese and Japanese as well as "The Three Little Pigs" and "Three Little Kittens"? For, in fact, the three-year-old's desire to be heard can express itself as easily in Japanese as it can in doggerel, and without trace of accent.

Just who *is* Masaru Ibuka to tell us that such marvelous things are possible? What are his credentials for making such statements? His credentials are impeccable.

1. He knows nothing about education, and therefore he does not know what can and cannot be done. (An absolute requirement for making a staggering breakthrough in an established field.)

2. He is an unqualified genius. (Beginning in 1947 when his own nation was desolated, with three very young men to help and a capital of $700, he established a firm which he called Sony. He was among a handful of pioneers who brought Japan from physical ruin and spiritual despair to a position of leadership in the world.)

3. He is doing what he proposes should be done. (As executive director of the Early Development Association in Tokyo and as a director of Talent Education in Matsumoto, he is presently giving thousands of Japanese children opportunity to learn and to do the things described.)

Mr. Ibuka does *not* propose to change the system of education and as a consequence change what a child learns.

Mr. Ibuka proposes to change how a child is given opportunity to learn and as a consequence to change the system of education.

All the evidence indicates that the former cannot be done to any important degree.

The latter is presently occurring.

Are these things possible, or are they the rosiest sorts of dreams? They are both, because I have seen all these things over and over again around the world.

I have seen newborns swim with the Timmermans in Australia. I have seen four-year-olds speak English with Dr. Honda in Japan. I have seen small children do advanced gymnastics with the Jenkins in the United States. I have seen three-year-olds play the violin and the grand piano with Dr. Suzuki in Matsumoto. I have seen a three-year-old read three languages with Dr. Veras in Brazil. I have seen two-year-old Sioux children ride full-grown horses in South Dakota. I have seen three-year-olds read Kanji, the language of the scholars in Japan. I have letters from thousands of mothers the world over who wrote in the most charming of terms to tell me of the wonderful things that happened to their two-year-olds after they taught them to read, using my book *How to Teach Your Baby to Read.*

I think that Mr. Ibuka's gentle book is one of the most important books ever written, and I believe it should be read by every parent alive.

Instead of introducing this book with the highest praise I am able to summon, I should hate Mr. Ibuka for writing it. All my life I have prepared myself for writing two books, and to write them has been the goal of my life. The first of the books I have spent my life preparing to write is on the subject of the fantastic ability of tiny children to learn anything easily and joyfully. The second book I am going to write is on the subject of *how* to make every child physically, intellectually, and emotionally superior.

It is no longer necessary for me to write the first book: this industrialist has already written it, and the reader presently has it in his hands.

It is now absolutely necessary that I end this introduction so that the reader can get to one of the most delightful and important books he has ever read, and so that I can get back to writing that second book before Masaru Ibuka, the industrialist and authority on how children learn, beats me to writing the second book as well.

GLENN DOMAN
Director
The Institutes for the Achievement of
Human Potential
Philadelphia, Pennsylvania

Introduction

It has generally been accepted from ancient times that exceptional talent or genius is largely due to heredity, a freak of the genes. When we are told that the musical saint Mozart gave a piano performance at age three, or that John Stuart Mill was able to read classical literature in Latin at the same age, most of us tend to conclude simply that "Of course, geniuses are born different."

Nevertheless, a close examination of these men's early years tells us that both Mozart and Mill had been strictly trained by fathers who were oriented to an extraordinary degree to the education of their children. It is my proposition that neither Mozart nor Mill was born a genius; but that each was provided from his earliest years with the education and environment to develop his talent to the very utmost.

In contrast, a newborn baby brought up in an environment essentially hostile to his or her needs has no chance later in life of developing fully. An extreme example is the famous story of the "wolf girls," Amala and Kamala, found in a cave in the 1920s southwest of Calcutta, India, by a missionary couple who made great efforts to restore the children, reared by wolves, to their original humanity, but in vain.

We take it for granted that a child born of a human being is human and a creature born of a wolf, wolf. However, these two children continued to display the characteristics of the wolf. It was thus the kind of education and environment of the infant right after birth that seemed to determine whether it was to become a human being or a wolf!

Pondering these examples, I could not help thinking more and more deeply about the great influence that education and environment have on newborn babies. The question came to assume the utmost importance, not just for individual children, but for the health and happiness of society at large, so in 1969 I was instrumental in setting up a foundation called the Early Development Association in Japan. Research workers, both native and foreign, assembled together to study; and at the same time we opened experimental classes to analyze, expand, and apply Dr. Shinichi Suzuki's method of teaching small children to play the violin, which was then attracting the attention of the world.

As we have proceeded with this work, we have been made increasingly aware of how wrong has been much traditional thinking about children in their earliest years. We assume that we know all about children; yet we know very little about their real potential. We pay a great deal of attention to what should be taught to children after the age of three; yet by then, according to recent studies of cerebral physiology, the development of human brain cells is 70 to 80 percent completed. Is it not therefore to the years *before* three, when the brain is developing, that we should devote our efforts?

"Early development" is not a proposal for force-feeding tiny children with facts and figures. It is an approach to education *preceding* schooling, and its keynote is the introduction of new experience at the "appropriate time." It is only those who have the day-to-day care of the young child, usually mothers, who can discover this time. So I have written this book in the hope of being of help to these mothers, and I pray that it may serve to help make more wonderful adults of the children now being born.

MASARU IBUKA

Part I

INFANT POTENTIALITY

THE IMPORTANT PERIOD

Kindergarten Is Too Late

Everyone must have had the experience, in his or her own school days, of seeing an exceptionally gifted pupil maintain his place at the top of the class without any obvious effort, while the class slow learner made no improvement however desperately he tried.

In my day teachers used to encourage us by saying, "Whether or not you are intelligent is not a question of heredity. It all depends on your efforts." Yet our own experience clearly demonstrated that a bright one is always bright and a stupid one, always stupid. Intelligence did indeed seem to have been determined from the very beginning. What were we to make of the contradiction?

I have come to the conclusion that man's ability and character are not determined by birth, but are fairly well formed by a certain period in his life. There have long been controversies over whether man's being is shaped by heredity or by the kind of education he receives after birth, but no convincing theory has been able to settle the matter—until recently.

At last, however, the study of cerebral physiology on the one hand and infant psychology on the other has made it possible to show that the key to the development of intelligence is in the child's experience

19

of the first three years—that is, during the period of development of the brain cells. No child is thus born a genius, and none is born a fool. All depends on the stimulation of the brain cells during the crucial years.

These years are the years from birth to three. Kindergarten is too late.

Any Child Can Do Well—It All Depends on the Method of Education

Readers may well wonder why I, an engineer by training and now company president, should happen to step into the field of early development. My reasons are partially "public"—that is, I find myself deeply concerned about the present rebellions of the young, and asking myself how far our present education has contributed to their discontent; and partly private— I have a child who is mentally retarded. While this child was going through the early developing stages, I was totally ignorant of the idea that a child born with such a heavy burden could develop to a remarkable degree, if properly educated from birth. What opened my eyes was the claim of Dr. Shinichi Suzuki that "any child will do well—it all depends on the method of educating." When I witnessed in person the remarkable results of Dr. Suzuki's "Talent Education" method of teaching the violin to very young children, I could not help regretting that I as a parent had not been able to do anything for my own child.

When I first considered the phenomenon of the student rebellions in Japan, I gave a great deal of thought to the meaning of education, and why it was that our system produces so much aggression and discontent. At first, the problem seemed to me to be in the system of university education. However, as my thinking progressed further, it seemed already to exist in high school. Then I went even further back to middle and elementary schools, and I finally reached the conclusion that it is too late to influence the child in kindergarten. This thinking coincided unexpectedly with what Dr. Suzuki and his associates had been practicing.

Dr. Suzuki has been teaching his unique "Suzuki Method" for the past thirty years. Before that, he had taught elementary and high school children in accordance with the generally accepted modes of education. He found that the difference between those children who make progress and those who don't is very conspicuous, so he decided to experiment with younger children, then still younger, and he kept on lowering the age level of those he taught. Dr. Suzuki teaches violin, but that is because he happens to be a violinist. The realization that his method could be applied to any field prompted me to involve myself seriously in "early development."

Early Development Is Not for Producing Geniuses

I have often been asked, "Does early development try to produce geniuses?"

The answer is "No." The only purpose of early development is to educate a child to attain a flexible mind and a healthy body, and to be bright and gentle.

All men, unless physically handicapped, are born the same. If there are divisions among children into intelligent groups and dull-minded groups, and gentle groups and belligerent groups, the responsibility lies with upbringing. Any child, provided he is given what he should be given at a proper stage in his life, should grow up with a bright mind and a solid character.

A boy criminal who shocked the world several years ago by committing a series of senseless murders with a pistol wrote a diary in prison. He said in it: "I hear that one's personality and character are formed by the time one is five years old. Five years in man's lifetime is only a short time (a few years and months). But if it forms a character which influences his whole life to this degree, what important years they are, and how negligent parents are."

For me the fundamental purpose of early development is to keep the world from producing unfortunate children such as this one. The goal of inducing an infant to listen to good music and take lessons in violin is not to make a musical genius of the child; the goal of having him learn a foreign language is not to make a linguistic genius of him, or to prepare him for admission to a "good" kindergarten and elementary school. They are strictly means to bring out the infinite potential of the child, to increase his joy in himself and in the world.

The Very Immaturity of Human Babies Points to Great Potentiality

My thinking about early development starts with the idea of the infinite potential a newborn baby has.

A newborn baby is, of course, totally helpless; but

it is precisely because he is so helpless that his potential is so great. The state in which a human infant is born is far less developed than that of any other baby animal: it is only the human baby that knows no more than how to cry and suck milk. Other animal babies, such as a dog, a monkey, or a horse, can crawl, cling, or even immediately stand up and walk. The zoologists claim that the human baby is behind other animal babies by ten to eleven months, and one reason for this difference is said to be the walking posture of man. Once man started to walk in an erect posture, a fetus could no longer stay in the mother's body until its development was complete, so it is born while still in a state of utter helplessness. It has to learn to use its limbs after birth. And it has similarly to learn to use its brain. Whereas the brain of any other baby animal is almost formed by the time of birth, the brain of the human baby is still like a blank piece of paper.

What abilities a child is to have depend entirely on what is to be written on this blank paper.

Circuits of the Brain Are Formed by the Age of Three

The brain cells of human beings are said to amount to 1.4 billion in number, but most of the brain cells of a newborn baby are not yet in operation. Recent research indicates that the "operative cells" will have been found, however, by the age of three.

Individual brain cells are all separate at birth, and they cannot function individually at all. A microscopic photograph of the brain cells taken right after birth shows that as time goes on and the brain develops, protuberances come increasingly into being, connecting one cell to another, like bridges. That is, brain cells stretch out their hands to one another and then link and cling together, to respond to and correlate information received from outside through the senses. This process is exactly like the working of the transistors in an electronic computer. No individual transistor can function by itself, but it is when connected by a circuit to other transistors, all the transistors together function as an electronic computer.

The period when the brain cells learn most rapidly to make these connections is the period between birth and three years of age. Seventy to eighty percent of the connections are formed by the age of three. And as these connections develop, the capacity of the brain increases. In the first six months after birth, the brain capacity has reached 50 percent of its adult potential, and by age three, 80 percent. This, of course, does not mean that the brain cells of the child after age three stop developing: it is the rear part of the brain that develops by the age of three, and at about age four, a different part of the brain begins to go through a wiring process. This is the front part, called the "frontal lobes." The difference is in the wiring process during the periods before and after the age of three and is equivalent to the development first of the hardware of the equipment, which is the main circuitry of the machine, and then to the software, which determines the way in which the equipment is used.

The fundamental facility of the brain to catch stimuli from outside, make patterns of them, and then remember is the "hardware," the facility on which all further development depends. Such advanced capacities as thinking, willing, creating, and feeling develop after the age of three; but they use the faculty already formed by that age.

Therefore, unless the "hardware" formed in the first three years is sound, there is no point in repeatedly attempting to train the "how to use" activity in later years; just as there is no point in trying to operate an electronic computer of poor quality and expect to achieve good results.

Shyness in a Baby Is a Proof of Development in His Pattern-Cognitive Faculty

I would like to explain here the particular use to be made in this book of the word "pattern."

The English word "pattern" is most frequently used to mean a "design," an "arrangement of form," or a "model." However, I propose to use this word in a broader but more specialized sense, to denote a process of thinking, the process by which the infant brain recognizes and correlates information. Whereas an adult grasps information mainly through his reasoning faculty, the child uses his intuition, his unique facility for making an instant pattern; adult reasoning is not easily acceptable to the infant, and must come later.

The most impressive evidence of this early pattern-cognitive faculty is the tiny baby's ability to recognize different faces. I particularly remember a baby at a special children's institution, which a friend of mine was running, who was said to have been able to identify fifty different adult faces by the time he was one year and a few months old. Furthermore, he not only recognized them but gave each of them a nickname, calling this one "Boo-boo chan" ("chan" is an affectionate and familiar form of address in Japanese) and that one "Wa-wa chan."

"Fifty people" may sound easy, but it is very difficult for an adult to remember fifty new faces in the course of a year. It is impossible to do this difficult and complicated task through reasoning; just try to write down the distinct features of all the people with whom you are acquainted, and see if you can distinguish them one from another analytically.

The infant's superior pattern-cognitive faculty begins to be clearly evident about half a year after birth, when shyness begins to show itself. His small brain can now distinguish familiar faces such as his father's and mother's from those that are strange to him, and he makes clear his awareness by rejecting the stranger.

Current Education Mistakes a Period of "Strictness" for a Period of "Permissiveness"

Even today many psychologists and educators, particularly those who are said to be "progressive," see it as a sin to try consciously to "educate" a small child. They say that to stuff a small head with information only creates an anxious child, and that it is natural to leave the child to grow up in his own way. Some even think it natural that the young child should be selfish, acting only at his pleasure. Thus parents throughout the world, influenced by this thinking, conscientiously follow the "let-alone" principle.

Yet once their children are in kindergarten or in school, these same parents often abandon their "let-alone" policy, and start to be strict in training and educating them. All of a sudden, "gentle" mothers change into "fearsome" mothers.

That this is a reversal of the proper order of development should be evident from the previous discussion on the development of the human brain cells. Instead, I would wish to see a mother during her child's first years as a true "education-mama"— which is the term used in Japan to ridicule mothers who push and bully their children throughout their schooling.

For it is during the very early years that one must be at once strict and gentle with one's child; and after that, when the child starts developing his own self, one should gradually begin to respect his self and will. To put the idea in its extreme form, parental interference should be over before the kindergarten age. Not to intervene during the proper years and then to start to interfere with the child once he is in kindergarten can only kill his talent and stimulate rebellion in him.

WHAT A SMALL CHILD CAN DO

Adult Concepts of "Difficult" and "Easy" Do Not Hold True for Young Children

We adults are liable to say, "This book is too difficult for a child," or "A baby can't possibly appreciate classical music"; but on what basis do we make such judgments as these? To children, free of preconceived ideas of what is "difficult" or "likable," the impact of the English language or the Japanese language, Bach's music or children's songs, monophonic music or harmony, must all start from exactly the same point: that is, they all are entirely new.

A judgment derived from the senses is not dependent on knowledge; on the contrary, in one sense knowledge can be an obstacle to judgment. When seeing a so-called "famous painting" many people must have had the experience of saying to themselves, "This famous painting is wonderful" without really having been deeply moved, simply because the name of the painter and the price attached to the painting indicated such an evaluation. In contrast, a small child is honest. He becomes engrossed in an object or experience that stimulates and appeals to his senses to the point of losing his entire self in the object.

The educational television program for preschool children called *Sesame Street*, in which most of the characters are puppets, and the main setting is Harlem in New York City, is extremely popular. The interesting thing about this program is that each character has a definite personality, characteristic of a real person found in any neighborhood. One might imagine that a two-year-old child could not appreciate the diversity in these characters, but this has proved not to be so. Every child has a favorite character of his own, and whenever this character appears on the screen the child becomes absorbed in the story as if it were his own. The character that is most popular is a very large bird. He is a bit frivolous and makes many mistakes, but he is innocent and open-minded; and in addition, he never forgets to try to learn. Children identify themselves with him immediately and spontaneously.

The fact that a child too young to speak his own language coherently can understand the complex personalities of these puppets as well as an adult can, or even better, is very important. It is in itself a repudiation of the adult concept that simple things are "for children" and complex things "not for children."

Small Children Can Remember "Pigeon" More Easily Than "Nine"

I recall an occasion when my two-year-old grandson visited me for the first time in a long while. Looking out the window and pointing out to me various neon signs, he told me very proudly, "This is Hitachi and that is Toshiba." Trying to hide the delight I could not help feeling that he, my own grandson, at the age of two could read "Hitachi" and "Toshiba" in

Chinese characters, I asked his mother, "When did he learn Chinese characters?"

It turned out that my grandson was not reading "Hitachi" and "Toshiba" in Chinese characters, but remembering the trademarks as patterns and thus identifying the "Hitachi" and "Toshiba" neon signs. There was a great deal of laughter at me for being a "foolish, doting grandfather," but I am sure many people have had such an experience.

Just the other day I received a letter from a twenty-eight-year-old mother living in Fujisawa who had read a series of articles I had written on early development for some weekly magazine. According to her letter, her eldest son, two and a half years old, had started remembering shapes of cars when he was about two and within a few months could easily name about forty different cars, both Japanese-made and foreign-made, and in some cases he could tell the name of a car even when it was under a covering in the parking place. Just before or after this incident, probably influenced by television programs about Expo 70, he had started remembering flags of various countries, and now he could identify and name correctly the flags of thirty countries, including the flags of Mongolia, Panama, and Lebanon—flags that adults have difficulty in identifying. This incident points to a facility among young children which adults no longer have, and therefore have great difficulty in imagining. The infant is endowed with a wonderful ability to recognize certain kinds of things in terms of a pattern. This facility has nothing to do with analyzing or theorizing, which the child learns to do only much later. An outstanding example is the ability of a few-months-old baby to identify his mother's face. Many babies start crying when they are held by strangers, but stop crying and smile when held by their own mothers. They may, of course, in part be simply responding to their mother's affection, but they are also remembering as patterns the face of the mother and the way in which she holds her child.

According to an experiment conducted by Mr. Isao Ishii, who gives lessons in Chinese characters for our Early Development Association, a three-year-old child has no difficulty in remembering very complex Chinese characters, such as "pigeon" and "giraffe." The point is that to a young child who remembers without much effort subtle differences in facial expression, the complex identification of Chinese characters is not a problem at all. In contrast to abstract words such as "nine," words naming concrete objects such as "giraffe," "raccoon," and "fox" he can easily remember, however complex they may be. So it is no mystery that the child can beat a grown-up at card games such as hearts or rummy. Whereas the adult has to memorize places, numbers, and signs with conscious effort, the child has a wonderful capacity to remember instantly by recognition of patterns.

Small Children Can Understand Algebra More Easily Than "Crane-Tortoise" Arithmetic

A fundamental idea in modern mathematics is the theory of "sets," which for adults, who were first taught the concept of number, and then geometry, and then algebra, is not at all easy to grasp. However, to the small child, the logic of the "sets," or "multiple," theory is apparently readily understandable, and according to Madame Richenne Félix, a French authority on the teaching of mathematics, the child can never be too young to be taught it.

Since a "set," or "multiple," is simple a collection of things that have some quality in common, the toddler is in fact introduced to it when he starts to play with his building blocks, taking them one by one out of the box and distinguishing a square block from a triangular one. He already at that stage understands very well that each block is one element in a larger "set," and that the pile of square blocks forms a smaller set and the triangular ones another. This very simple idea, that objects can be sorted into various groups according to varying characteristics, is the fundamental principle behind the theory of sets. So it is quite natural that the young child can understand the simple and logical reasoning of the multiple theory more easily than the complicated and weird logic of arithmetic.

I consider, then, that the traditional assumption that arithmetic is easy and algebra difficult is another of the preconceived errors of judgment that adults tend to make about children. Since the young child's brain easily understands the logic of the multiple theory, it is only a small step to understanding the logic of algebra.

Here is, for example, a "crane-tortoise" mathematical problem: "Here are several cranes and tortoises [or perhaps, for American children, birds and cats]—a total of eight altogether. The number of their legs together totals twenty. How many cranes and how many tortoises are there?"

First, let us solve this problem by algebra. We say that X stands for the number of cranes and Y for the number of tortoises; so $X + Y = 8$, and $2X + 4Y$ (the

number of legs) = 20. By cancellation we find that
$X + 2Y = 10$. Since $X = 8 - Y$, therefore $Y = 2$: there are
two tortoises (and thus six cranes).

Now let us solve the same problem by "crane-tortoise" arithmetic. If we suppose that all are tortoises,
the number of legs would be 32. However, the number
of legs given is 20 and therefore there are 12 extra
legs in the proposition. There are 12 extra legs because we have assumed that all are tortoises, which
have 4 legs, whereas in reality some are cranes that
have only 2 legs. So the extra 12 is the number of
cranes multiplied by the difference in the leg-number
between the two animals: 12 divided by 2 is 6, which
is the number of cranes present, and the 2 left over
when we subtract 6 from 8, the total number of animals, is the number of tortoises.

Why do we have to solve a problem with such a
complicated method as "crane-tortoise" arithmetic,
when we have a logical and straightforward way of
getting the answer by substituting X and Y for un-
known numbers?

Although the way to solve a problem in algebra
may not come quickly, the logical reasoning of algebra is far easier to understand than illogical reasoning, seemingly easy at first glance.

Even an Infant Can "Appreciate" a Bach Suite

In the Atsugi Sony Factory a kindergarten has been
established for children whose mothers are working.
Some time ago a survey was conducted there to find
out what kind of music the children liked. It revealed
truly unexpected results.

The music about which the children were most enthusiastic proved to be Beethoven's Fifth Symphony! Popular songs such as are broadcast on television from morning till night were second in popularity, and the songs written for children were least popular. I became greatly interested in these results.

The young children found sophisticated classical music, which we adults often keep at a respectful distance, most interesting. Are children endowed with the musical sense necessary for appreciating a complex symphony right from the beginning? According to experiments conducted by Dr. Shinichi Suzuki, a five-month-old baby can appreciate a Vivaldi concerto. And this brings to mind a story told me by a young couple of my acquaintance.

This couple, themselves lovers of classical music, had their baby listen soon after birth to Bach's Suite No. 2 for a few hours every day. In three months, the baby started to move his body in a lively fashion according to the rhythm. As the rhythm quickened toward the climax, the baby's movements became rapid and more active, and when the music came to an end, he showed his displeasure. Often, when the baby was feeling cross or crying, his parents would put this music on and he would be soothed immediately. One day, on the other hand, when the parents put on some discordant jazz music, the baby started crying violently. When I heard this story, I again marveled at the wonder that an infant should be so musically sensitive as to appreciate a Bach suite.

I am not saying that any classical music is by definition good, but I am saying that the capacity to appreciate complex musical forms directly through the senses (intuitively) is a wonder. The reason that many of us Japanese cannot appreciate Western classical music is probably simply that we heard nothing but children's songs and Japanese folk songs during our infancy.

A Young Baby Can Even Swim

There are many fully grown men who don't know how to swim (they "sink like a hammer," as we say in Japanese). So you may be surprised to know that a tiny baby can swim if taught. A baby who has not yet used his legs for walking treats floating in the water as he treats crawling on the ground: as another new activity. The important thing is not that *even* a baby can swim—he can swim *because* he is a baby.

Some years ago I came across a newspaper article about a Belgian named de Beneseil who had opened a swimming school for babies. According to de Beneseil, a baby at three months could be trained in the pool to float on his back, and by nine months could learn to breathe correctly in the water.

Later, in August 1965, Rizet Deem, president of the International Women's Athletic Conference, held in Tokyo, talked about teaching a baby under a year old to swim, thus creating a considerable sensation.

Mrs. Deem described how she had introduced a five-month-old baby to a pool at a temperature of 32° Celsius (90° Fahrenheit) and how within three months he could swim by himself for an average of six minutes at a time. Even more surprising, his record swim had lasted eight minutes forty-six seconds. At a press conference, Mrs. Deem said, "A baby knows how to balance himself far better in the water than on the ground. First you support the baby in the water with your hands, and when the baby becomes accustomed to the feel of the water, he begins to float by himself. Even when his face goes under the water, he waits, with his eyes closed and holding his breath, until his body floats to the surface of the water. Then he learns to move forward using his hands and legs." Mrs. Deem insisted repeatedly on the possibility of starting to develop all human abilities and talents before the baby is a year old.

That an infant can swim is only one more indication of the infinite potential in the human baby. It has also been reported that a child just learning to walk can learn to roller-skate at the same time, for he acquires new skills indiscriminately: walking, swimming, and sliding, all belong equally in the realm of new experience, and he treats them all, if properly encouraged, with the same sense of adventure.

Needless to say, these various experiments are not being done merely for the purposes of teaching swimming and violin to tiny tots. Swimming is only a means to developing the infant's potential—by giving him a good night's rest and a good appetite, by sharpening his reflexes, and by strengthening his muscles. "Strike while the iron is hot," it is said: in other words, it is too late to strike and mold the iron after it has cooled and hardened. Molding and forming the material before it becomes rigid results in the desired strong and high-quality product.

A Small Child's Brain Can Take an Almost Infinite Amount of "Input"

"Brother and sister, linguistic geniuses who understand five languages, and their 'aggressive' father."

Many Japanese will remember this headline in a national newspaper. The "aggressive father" is Mr. Masao Nagata, who resigned from a long teaching career and, calling himself a homemaker, devoted himself to the education of his children with his whole body and soul. The son was then two and a half years old and the daughter, a three-month-old baby. Because of their very young ages, a number of angry criticisms were directed against this "aggressive education-papa."

Some complained that it was a pity to cram the children's heads indiscriminately, that this was too big a burden for the children, and that they would in consequence grow up overanxious.

That the Nagatas are now living quietly in good health and vigor is enough to prove, I think, that these criticisms were all quite off the point. So is the question of whether it is right or wrong for a father to retire into the household and take on the responsibility of educating his children. What is important is that the method of education that Mr. Nagata used offers us some very important hints about the infant's potentiality for learning. The following is what Mr. Nagata said about his unique method of instruction:

I started teaching English, English conversation, Italian, German, and French . . . almost at once. When you listen to the foreign-language program on the radio, a French lesson is sometimes explained in English. So I thought that if you taught many languages at once, you could link them together. Just then the children were taking piano lessons, and the music they happened to be practicing had the tempo markings written in Italian and the explanation in English, German, and French.

Unless they understood the explanation, they would not grasp the music. That was one of the reasons for my teaching languages.

I was often asked if the children were not confused by studying five languages all at once, but they were able to use them each in their right and proper way. For language study, I used nothing but radio programs. These programs are conducted in a very kind manner. Pronunciation practices are carried on in a courteously slow way. Then the children opened their mouths and practiced pronunciation very properly.

(from *Early Development,* May, 1970)

It seems that the absorbing capacity of the small child's brain is far greater than that of a grown-up man. Therefore, there is no ground for concern about "force-feeding" or overstimulating him: like a sponge, the young child's brain absorbs, and if it comes to a point of saturation, it automatically stops taking any more in.

What we should now be concerned about is not offering the child too much, but not giving him enough. Mr. Nagata has proved it to us by his experiment.

The Child Remembers Only What He Is Interested in

I have so far discussed the wonderful ability of the young child's brain to absorb. Of course, his brain at this stage is simply a machine for receiving what is given, and it does not have the capacity for selecting, discriminating, and understanding. What is given to the child is distributed exactly as it is through the brain, as in a computer through wires.

However, there soon comes a time when the child develops the desire to make a decision of his own; in short, there comes a time when that part of the brain develops which decides how to use the hardware that has already been made. This time is usually said to be around the age of three. This is the time when the question of how to interest the child becomes more important than what should be offered him. The child remembers whatever interests him to a point of greediness. During this process the capacities to will, to create, and to want to do something are developed, all having important functions in shaping the brain for later activities and in forming character.

All parents read children's stories and fairy tales to their children regardless of whether or not the child understands them. After hearing them many times, the young child knows them by heart and is quick to point out mistakes in the parent's careless reading. The child remembers children's stories and fairy tales with great precision, but this is a precision based more on apprehension of patterns than on understanding.

Then the child begins to show a special interest in one particular story and wants to read it by himself. Although he does not know how to read the alphabet, he compares the story he has memorized with the pictures in the book and reads the story, smoothly following the words that he cannot yet read. This is the period when the child starts asking insistently for the meanings of various words. That he asks persistently is a proof of his great interest.

One mother I know seized this opportunity very

skillfully by encouraging her child's natural interest in Chinese characters. This mother bought from a secondhand-book store in Kanda a fairy-tale book with the Japanese alphabet alongside Chinese characters, and she read it again and again to the child, looking at the book together with him. In a short while, he had the whole story memorized, and when he started to read by himself, he took an interest in Chinese characters. The mother taught him Chinese characters one by one as the child asked about them. She responded only to his curiosity, so there was no question of his feeling burdened. He soon could recognize the Chinese characters he saw in a newspaper his father was reading, thus causing much excitement in the house; and he was able to read most of the newspaper's content before entering school.

Thus, the child before the age of three has no difficulty in learning what he is interested in, no matter how much effort and concentration this may require of him.

Many Skills Are Impossible to Acquire Unless Learned Very Early

There are frequently occasions in my business life when I have to speak in English. What always troubles me on such occasions is the faultiness of my English pronunciation and intonation. It is not that the listener does not at all times understand my Japanized English—he does. But I sometimes face a moment when the listener asks me with a puzzled look to repeat something, and I have to spell out a word in English so as to be understood, feeling very sorry about my "good*o* morning"–type English.

In contrast to this, a boy in my neighborhood, aged one year and two months, can pronounce English words with perfect accuracy. Such sounds as *r* and *l* are very difficult for most Japanese to distinguish, but he does it correctly. Probably the difference stems from the fact that while I started studying English for the first time in junior high school, this boy, having been already familiar with English by listening to records in that language, started to learn English conversation from an American lady friend at just about the same time he was beginning to speak Japanese.

All this means that once the pattern of the mother tongue is formed in one's mind, it is very difficult to take in the patterns of a different language later on. However, as I explained earlier, the brain of the child under the age of three is still in the process of being "wired," and the "circuitry" for the native language and that for another language can easily be developed at the same time. Therefore, children at this age can without much effort speak any language as though it were their own. If one should miss this period, one has to struggle through in order to acquire what comes so naturally to the young child, and even then what one acquires is less than the facility so easily learned at the right time. Most adults and older children will never be able to speak a foreign language correctly with perfect pronunciation.

Foreign languages are not the only facilities it is too late to acquire after the early developing years. For instance, one's sense of absolute pitch and one's athletic sense—one's physical coordination and balance—are said to be formed by this age. And the basis for aesthetic appreciation—the sensory response—is developed around the same time.

Every year, at the beginning of the summer vacation, foreign families bring their young children to Dr. Suzuki's violin class. Needless to say, at first no one speaks a word of Japanese. The youngest children are the first to start speaking it; next come the brothers and sisters in elementary and junior high schools. The hopeless ones are their parents. Whereas within one month the children speak excellent Japanese, the parents have to take their children along with them as interpreters wherever they go, and there are many mothers and fathers who go back to their native countries knowing how to say only one word, "konnichiwa" (good day or hello), after a month's stay in Japan.

Early Development Enables a Child Hard of Hearing to Hear

Up to this point I have discussed from various angles the wonderful latent potential of the normal child, and the importance of early education for developing this potential. However, there are unfortunately many infants throughout the world handicapped by the effects of polio, mental retardation, deafness, and dumbness. Early development is not unconcerned about these infants: on the contrary, by reason of their heavy burden, it is essential to identify their handicap as early as possible, so as to use the techniques of early development to compensate for it as far as possible.

What I am about to tell you is a moving story taken from a recent newspaper article: the story of a child born deaf who was later able to participate in daily conversation without difficulty, owing to the great efforts of his parents. Upon reading this, I was encouraged, thinking of this as a true example of early development.

Atsuto, now aged six, was born an apparent embodiment of health. He was a year old before his parents noticed any abnormality. They asked themselves whether there was anything wrong with his hearing ability, but they did not worry very much at this stage, thinking simply that there are many children who are slow to talk, and their child was one of them. But when Atsuto was still silent at the age of a year and a half, they finally took him to a hospital for an examination. The diagnosis proved that he was so hard of hearing as to be almost totally incapacitated. Not knowing what to do, the parents set about searching for help and finally found Dr. Takeshi Matsuzawa, an expert on the treatment and education of infants with hearing difficulty. Dr. Matsuzawa began by teaching the child his own name through a hearing aid. Then the child started to learn other words, one by one, the doctor insistently connecting words to meanings, and developing whatever traces of hearing the child did have. Dr. Matsuzawa believes that at the right age the deaf child can actually be *taught* to hear.

He writes:

It is only the mother who can quickly discover whether her child is abnormal. One week after birth, a baby responds to a loud noise or sound with a jumping motion. In a few months, the baby recognizes his mother's voice, and in four months, his own name. If the baby shows no response to a big noise or to the calling of his name, you can assume that something is wrong with his hearing. The child also comes to learn most of the words used in daily conversation by the age of three, so these early years are the most suitable for a child hard of hearing to learn words. What one should most avoid is keeping the child away from sounds just because he apparently cannot hear them. It is not true that even a very deaf child is utterly incapable of hearing. Have the child listen repeatedly to a sound, and he will develop an ability to hear.

Parental effort and education can thus make it possible to develop the ability to hear even if the child is born with a hearing difficulty. This is exactly what constitutes the theory of early development.

Part II

THE IMPACT OF EARLY EXPERIENCE

It Is Environment That Counts, Not Genes

In the last section, I talked about the wonderful latent potential of the very young child. Whether the latent buds grow into a strong tree or a beautiful flower depends on the way you cultivate your child and the kind of environment you create for him. In this section I am going to discuss in concrete detail the practical side of early development, but before I start I would like to offer some evidence that education and environment do indeed take precedence over heredity in the development of young children.

Professor Benjamin Bloom at the University of Chicago once compared the IQ of a child brought up on a kibbutz in Israel with that of an African child who had emigrated there. The result showed that the IQ of the Israeli child was 115 compared with 85 for the African child, revealing a marked difference between them. Bloom concluded that this difference was due to differences in race and extraction between the African and the Israeli: that is, that ability is innately superior, or inferior, before education and environment have any influence.

Subsequently, a man named Ford did an experiment over a longer period of time. He took care of an immigrant couple from Africa, had their baby go to a nursery school immediately after birth, and brought him up in exactly the same environment as an Israeli child. The IQ of this African child at the age of four turned out to be 115, as high as that of the Israeli child.

Thus Ford's experiment refuted the theory that ability is determined genetically and became famous for its direct revelation that human ability is in fact determined by education and environment after birth.

In Japan there have been several experiments on identical twins brought up in different homes from the time of birth. The actual results have proved that even children with identical heredity, if brought up in different surroundings and taught by different people, will differ considerably in character as well as in talents and abilities.

The problem is, what kind of education and environment best develops the potential of the infant? On this point scholars have tried various methods and situations and reported on their results. There are also parents who, not quite satisfied with school education, have dared to experiment with the education of their own children. And in addition, experiments that cannot be done with human children have been done with dogs and monkeys, and the results have often been illuminating. I would like to discuss some of these experiments now.

The Child of a Scholarly Father Will Not Necessarily Be Scholarly

I often hear mothers say, "My child must have taken after his father, for he has no musical sense" or "My husband is a writer, so our child is good at writing essays." Certainly, as the proverbs say, "A frog's child will be a frog," and "an onion will not produce a rose," and there have indeed been cases in which a scholar's child has become a scholar and a merchant's child, a merchant. These cases do not mean, however, that the children had the qualifications for these professions transmitted to them biologically. From the moment of birth, they were probably brought up in an environment that encouraged them to become what their fathers had been. The environment the parents provided became the environment of the child, cultivating his ability for his father's profession by arousing his interest in it.

If lineage were a determining factor in forming the child's ability, it must necessarily follow that for generations children would succeed to their fathers' professions. But life is much more interesting than that, for it is not rare for a scholar's child to become a violinist or a doctor's child, a writer. Neither Mr. Kouji Toyoda, presently concertmaster of the Berlin Radio Symphony Orchestra, for instance, nor Mr. Kenji Kobayashi, concertmaster of the Oklahoma Symphony, had a famous musician as parent or relative. The environments in which they were brought up have made them what they are today.

One has only to look around one's own neighborhood to realize that a child born of talented parents is not necessarily talented. The world contemptuously calls a child like this "unworthy of his father"; but it can be said that the child is not responsible for what he is, as it is really the environment of his early years that has produced the "unworthy" child.

In contrast, a child born of an indolent, drunken father may often turn out to be an excellent engineer or artist. Despite the proverb that says "A kite has produced a hawk" (it is a case of the black hen's laying white eggs), such a child was not born with superior ability, but has rather been brought up in an environment that has enabled him to develop his talent. It is a case of a kite's creating an environment that was able to produce a hawk, rather than a case of a kite's producing a hawk.

Just as all babies are born with wrinkled faces, they are born alike in regard to ability and character, but they grow up to be different in both, owing to different environments and experiences.

In other words, the parent's profession and ability have no direct bearing on the formation of the child's ability and character. It can only be said that the reason that a doctor's child becomes a doctor is that he happens to be reared in surroundings where there are odors of medicines, people in white gowns, and patients.

A Human Baby Can Even Become an Animal If Brought Up Among Animals

A dog's child is a dog, a wolf's child, a wolf, and a human baby, a human being. This very natural fact may turn out to be not so natural, however, if one changes the environment, and I am about to tell you a true story to prove it. It is a famous story of the wolf girls, Amala and Kamala.

In October 1920 there spread rumors in a small village about 65 miles southwest of Calcutta, India, that two animals looking like human beings were living in a wolf cave. A missionary couple, Mr. and

Mrs. Synge, searched in the cave and caught the two animals, which were unquestionably two human beings, one conjectured to be eight and the other one and a half years old.

The two, apparently sisters, were named Kamala and Amala, and were placed in the charge of a local orphanage, where their education as human beings began.

The Synges tried with infinite affection and patience to implant in the sisters human characteristics and skills, but having been brought up by wolves during their early years, the children persistently behaved as wolves do. They crawled on hands and knees, and jumped at people who tried to touch them. They dozed off during daylight in a dark room, squatting down against the wall, and at night they started to howl. They ate only spoiled meat and live chickens.

Despite all this, the couple labored on, and eventually to some purpose, for within two months the younger sister, Amala, began babbling such words as "boo." However, she died within a year.

The older sister, after three years, was at long last able to start walking on two feet; however, whenever her instinctive reflex was precipitated she reverted to her old habit of walking on hands and knees. Throughout the nine years between her return to the human world and her death at the age of seventeen, her IQ remained that of a three-and-a-half-year-old child and her vocabulary never exceeded forty-five words.

More recently, a similar event took place in the jungle of Mozambique. A young African couple died, and their newborn baby disappeared.

A few months later, a human baby feeding at the breast of a female baboon was seen among a troop of baboons. Many attempts were made to get hold of the baby, but the effort eventually had to be abandoned.

In the following nineteen years, the baby grew up to be a strong young man who came to dominate the fierce baboons, as leader of the troop. Then, a few years ago, he was seized while sleeping in a tree. He was kept captive in a latticed hut, and attempts were made to train him in human ways. It has been reported that he eventually learned to eat using his hands and to walk on two feet.

The Small Child of Yesterday Is Completely Different Today

We do not take very exact note of how our own children are growing, for we see them every day. Yet they develop far more rapidly than we ever imagine. Professor Jean Piaget, the world-famous Swiss authority on developmental psychology, established his theory on phases of growth through observations of his three children, and the more I read his books the more acutely I feel the importance of providing a child with the education and environment proper to each of these phases.

According to Piaget's observation, a newborn baby sucks in everything that touches his lips, but within twenty days after birth, he will drink nothing but milk, and starts positively to demand it.

After three months, the baby begins to develop the will to reach out and touch something, such as the legs of a rag doll hung over the edge of a crib, taking much delight in it. And in one and a half years, the same child will find a way of touching something beyond the reach of his hand by using a stick. After two years of age he begins to connect words to abstract meanings, often in his own individual way— such as the word "man" with his father, or "rain" with street cleaning.

At around four years of age, the child still believes that the orange juice in a small glass filled to the brim is more than the same amount of orange juice in a large glass, and that cracker crumbs are more than a cracker in its uncrushed state. Only in his fifth to sixth year will he understand that the quantity in each case remains the same.

Thus, the child develops with amazing speed in both his mind and his body. This is all the more reason for him to be provided with suitable stimulation at every stage. To do this, parents need to observe carefully what he wants at what time, and what he is interested in, for it is the parents who are most closely in touch with him, and just as a proper time for learning a foreign language is important, there is an appropriate time for every step in early development.

To teach the child roller skating, for example, after he has learned to walk, is extremely difficult, but to teach him to skate at just about the same time as he is learning to walk makes a good roller skater of the child within a few months. Dr. Myrtle B. McGraw, an American psychologist, proved this point in an experiment with twin brothers. She taught one of them to skate eleven months after birth, and the other twenty-two months after birth, and found a marked difference in the results, the child who was taught earlier exhibiting much greater skill than the other.

Up to now, we have burdened our children unnecessarily by too often thinking that it was too early to teach them skills that could have been learned very easily had we recognized the proper time.

"As the Twig Is Bent So Grows the Tree"

I heard the following story from a young man who had just had a newborn baby girl when his company decided to send him abroad. His wife and child, therefore, went to live with his wife's parents in Tohoku.

When the young man returned from his one-year foreign duty, he and his wife and child went back to their apartment in Denen-Chofu in Tokyo and renewed their life as a family. At the time, the child was not yet able to speak much, but very soon she started to babble, and when she did the parents found themselves very much disconcerted. For all the words that came out of the child's mouth proved to be in Tohoku dialect. No matter how repeatedly the father said *"jidosha* (car)," for instance, in standard Japanese, the word the child pronounced as she imitated her father sounded like *"zudosha."* It was a very strange phenomenon indeed, for only the girl spoke Tohoku dialect, while everybody else in her family spoke nothing but standard Japanese.

It emerged that during the baby's stay in the home of his wife's parents, the grandparents, who adored her, had been with the baby constantly, talking and playing with her, and his wife, thinking that the child was still too little to speak, had left the matter as it was.

A few years later, when this child started school, she still could not rid herself of the Tohoku accent.

It seems that before the child began to speak, the distribution of the Tohoku dialect through "wires" in the brain had already taken place; and once completed, such a network is extremely difficult for a human being to destroy in order to begin anew. According to one theory, to begin a new circuit by destroying one already formed takes longer than it took to form the initial one.

As it is said in the proverb, "As the twig is bent so grows the tree": whatever influences a child in infancy makes the deepest possible impression, and it is up to the parents to make sure that the early influences are the right ones for that child.

A Room Devoid of Stimulation Is Harmful to a Baby

A bare room with pure white ceiling and walls, absolutely quiet with all the noises from outside shut out: a mother might think this environment ideal for her newborn baby. In fact such a room, devoid of stimulation, is not only useless but positively harmful to a baby.

According to an experiment performed by Professor Jerome S. Bruner in America, the degree of stimulation in the environment of a small baby makes a distinct difference in the development of the child's intelligence. He has proved this point through the following experiment. He first divided a number of babies into two groups, putting one group in a totally nonstimulating environment like the one described above. The other group was placed in a room with ceiling, walls, and blankets colorfully patterned with flowers, and through whose windows nurses and doctors could be seen at work. Music played in the background—it was a room filled with good stimulation.

The two groups were brought up in these different surroundings for a few months, after which tests were made to measure any differences in their intelligence. A shining object was offered to each child, and the length of time it took him to get hold of it was the measure by which the child's level of intelligence was determined. The results showed a clear three-month difference between the two groups: the level of intelligence of the group brought up in a room devoid of stimulation was three months behind that of the group placed in the other room.

This three-month lag at this particular stage is extremely important, because it is said that the development in intelligence from birth to three equals the development from ages four to seventeen. Some scholars claim that this lag can very soon be made up through proper training; but at the very least this means putting a great deal of pressure on a little child.

Experiments of this nature have been attempted not only by Professor Bruner, but by many other psychologists. The results show decisively that whether or not there is stimulation makes a difference in the development of ability.

Further study has focused on the kinds of stimulation most likely to promote the development of the child's intelligence. Rocking cradles, tassels with bright-colored fringe, shining balls, multicolored papers, and many other devices have been tested; a windmill attached to a music box and flower-patterned curtains, for instance, are said to have proved effective accelerants to development.

Professor Burton White of Harvard University, one of the psychologists involved in these experiments, claims that "We have clearly proved that provision of a rich environment achieves a remarkable effect on early development immediately after birth."

The Young Child Is Unexpectedly Influenced by Unexpected Things

Karl Friedrich Gauss is said to have been one of the greatest mathematicians of the nineteenth century; he discovered a formula for finding the sum of an arithmetical series when he was only eight years old. The reason I mention his name at this point is that I have recently found in a book some interesting facts about him.

Gauss's father was noted neither for his scholarship nor for anything else. He was a bricklayer who piled bricks one upon another in repairing walls, fences, and fireplaces. He always took his small son Karl with him wherever he went to do his work.

What little Karl did was sit down beside his father and hand him the bricks as he counted. Karl Gauss's mathematical ability, it is suggested in this book, must have been cultivated by this process during his early years.

I do not regard this interpretation as farfetched. I heard a similar story from Mr. Souichiro Honda, president of the Honda Engineering Company. When I asked him what had attracted him to motorcycles, he thought about it a while and told me the following story:

"In the olden days there were not even electric motors. People used oil motors for rice-cleaning. When I was little, there was a rice-cleaning mill near my house and I liked the *pom-pom* sounds of the oil motor. I used to go there just to see and hear it when I was so small that my grandfather carried me on his back. If I was not taken there, I would get cross and cry very hard. My crying was heard all over the neighborhood, so my grandfather reluctantly commuted there every day. Very soon, the *pom-pom* sound became as familiar to me as a lullaby, and I came to like even the odor of the exhaust gas. This could have been the cause of my attraction to motorcycles."

When I heard this, I thought that he was quite right. Early childhood must be like a delicate receiver. What parents regard as nonsensical and insignificant experiences, the child may receive with such sensitivity and intensity that the experience can prove to be the seed of a whole life. In this sense, the grandparent's seemingly insignificant habit of taking his grandson to see the oil motor gave birth to the world-famous king of motorcycles.

The Young Child May Read a Completely Different Story in a Picture Book from the Tale the Adult Reads

Difference in feeling and response between the young child and the adult becomes conspicuous when they come to read a picture book together. Madame Maria Montessori, the great Italian pioneer of infant education, has an example among her reports on early-childhood behavior. A certain mother gave to her one-and-a-half-year-old child some cards on which were printed various animals and hunting scenes. This toddler showed the cards to Madame Montessori and kept saying in his childish language a word that meant "car." She could not find among the cards any picture resembling a car, so she said questioningly, "There is no car"; but the boy answered, proudly pointing to a card, "Here it is." She looked hard at the card. It had beautiful pictures of a dog, a hunter, and a horse; and in the background at last she detected a dot on a line representing a road. The boy pointed to the dot and said, "car." It was unmistakably a minuscule car. The very minuteness of the depiction of the car must have fascinated the child.

Somewhere else, Madame Montessori gives an example of another one-and-a-half-year-old boy, whose mother had given him a picture book titled *Little Black Sambo* and was telling him the story.

"A little black boy named Sambo was walking along, carrying the presents given to him because it was his birthday. On the way he met wild animals and they robbed him of all the presents. He went home crying, but his parents comforted him. Feeling happy, he sat down in front of the dinner table, on which there was a birthday cake for him, as this last picture shows." When the mother finished the story, her little boy suddenly said, "No, he's crying." He pointed to the back of the cover, and there was printed a picture of Sambo in tears.

The small child, in other words, knows nothing about the conventions that adults have come to accept. His perceptions are immediate, and often, to adults, arbitrary—in dealing with children we need to learn to try to clear our own minds of preconceptions, and to use our imaginations to see as they see.

Leaving the Small Child in the Care of a Stranger Is Risky

I have heard a story like this. A pleasant and straightforward young couple had two boys, one aged five and the other four. While the younger one was popular in kindergarten for his liveliness and directness, the older one was rather spiritless and distinctly contrary. The parents were worried about the older child, not knowing what had made him so.

Quite at a loss, they eventually consulted a doctor, who in turn could not pinpoint a cause despite thorough investigation. However, after much discussion with the parents, he found that the older child at the age of a year had been left in the care of a nurse for six months, because the mother had been in bad health after giving birth to her second child.

The doctor guessed that if there was a single cause for the older son's present condition, it might go back to this period. He proceeded to get in touch with the nurse, and though reluctant at first, she started to talk bit by bit.

It turned out that when she had ostensibly been taking the child out for a walk, she had actually been meeting her lover in an old shed in the backyard. This had happened every day, and the child, then only a year old, had been left alone in the dark shed for two hours watching the rendezvous between the two.

How could this experience have failed to affect the

character formation of the child? Instead of bright sunshine and fresh air to stimulate him, he had had nothing but the humid air in the shed to cast a dark shadow over his soul and body. Needless to say, the one-year-old baby could not understand the meaning of the behavior between the nurse and her lover; but he would be only too aware of the girl's restless, guilty behavior, and of the rustling sounds coming from a dark corner, which must have communicated insecurity and fear to the child left alone there. It was this, the doctor concluded, that had made a timid and spiritless child of the boy.

On learning that, the parents were overcome with regret that they had left the child in the care of a stranger. We can sympathize indeed with the mother's weak physical condition after giving birth a second time within a year; but had they not been rather careless of the sensitive nature of the older baby? Circumstances may, of course, force people to leave their children in the hands of others. But I hope that my story shows how careful it is necessary to be in selecting those who are entrusted to look after children.

Early-Childhood Experience Becomes the Basis for Later Thinking and Doing

If one is asked to recount some incident in one's early childhood, one usually finds, unless the event has been exceptionally impressive, that one can really remember almost nothing. Even if one should recall happenings during the second or third year, one remembers them not as one's own experiences, but as stories told by one's mother or by other people around at the time.

Nevertheless, the fact that one does not remember early-childhood incidents does not mean that one has forgotten them. As I explained earlier, once it has in one way or another gone through the circuit-forming process in the brain, every experience and impression up to the age of three has become part of the foundation of the present self.

I am told that under hypnosis any person to whom it is suggested that he is now one year old will start speaking in year-old language and acting like a baby of that age. This means that every childhood experience is forever stored in the mind, once it has gone through the circuit-forming process in the brain, however impossible it may be to recall it.

It is also said that when man is driven to the last extremity, he suddenly relives the scenes of his early childhood. A politician, Mr. Kakuei Tanaka, has spoken of recalling his early childhood as it came back to him like a horse on a revolving carousel, when he wavered between life and death in a hospital during the war. He remembered being taken to a temple by his mother; the monk who had stood in front of the gate; and the monk's face, clothing, and manner of speaking—in complete and immediate detail. Later he told his mother about this "vision" and found out that it had actually happened when he was two years old.

Mr. Moriatsu Minato, president of the Nikko Research Center, was born in China, where he spent his early childhood. After that, however, he never spoke Chinese again and assumed he had forgotten it, until after many years he faced a situation in which he had to speak Chinese on a business trip to China. The Chinese language came flowing out of his mouth perfectly naturally and it was so fluent as to surprise both him and his Chinese hosts. After that, of course, the business discussions went smoothly.

This story shows once again how firmly early-childhood experiences are inscribed upon the brain, and emphasizes once more the fact that experience and environment up to the age of three underpin the thinking and doing of our present selves.

Unless the foundation is sturdy, it is useless to try to erect a sturdy building: even if the building is beautiful in appearance, it will crumble to pieces when touched by a gale or an earth tremor, if the foundation is not firm.

Early development is about this most important foundation-making. This foundation must be made very strong from the beginning, for it will be impossible to start laying foundations when the building is up.

Part III

WHAT IS GOOD FOR YOUNG CHILDREN?

There Are No Formulas for Infant Education

I have up to now been discussing the importance of environment for the small child, and the influence of early-childhood environment on the formation of his later being. In most families, it is the mother who carries on her shoulders the main responsibility for educating her child, but what I am about to say applies to anyone involved in the care of young children. In the first place, the mother should use plenty of her own initiative and imagination in educating her child according to his own stage of development. The detailed suggestions I am about to make should be treated as ideas on which the mother must form her own judgment and which she should accept or discard according to the particular nature or stage of development of the individual child.

Whenever I recommend that a very young child should listen to good music and see a real painting, I find myself approached by earnest mothers who want to know exactly what is meant by "good music" and a "real painting." Is Beethoven good, or Mozart? Van Gogh or Picasso? One might, of course, after consulting specialists, recommend specific music and paintings for children. However, what I want to offer is suggestions for parents to consider in relation to their own child, not a rigid program guaranteed to produce the perfect child. In education, particularly in infant education, there is no formula. Whatever the mother thinks is good for her child should be given to him without hesitation.

I think of this tendency to seek formulas as a serious defect in education: just because the child is five, he goes to kindergarten, and at the age of six he goes to elementary school. Such a policy based only on age ignores the young child's own level of ability. Japanese schools teach painting and numbers in kindergarten, "hiragana" (Japanese alphabet) in the first grade in elementary school, and Chinese characters in the second grade, on a pattern of educational thinking enslaved to the idea of a fixed program. We find the same response to the idea of early development: unless a strict formula is offered, no one dares to try it. I would prefer the notion that fixed ideas, formulas, and norms are *there to be defied.*

Holding the Baby Should Be Encouraged

A baby is feeling cross, Mother picks him up, and he stops crying and smiles: every parent throughout the world has experienced that situation, over and over again. But traditional wisdom has often been censorious of the mother who picks up her baby to soothe him—warning her against the "habit" of holding the infant constantly in her arms, and predicting that if a child is picked up whenever he cries, he will eventually never stop crying unless held. Is all this true? If these attitudes are taken simply as a warning against loving a child blindly, or "spoiling" him, I am willing to accept them. But I am firmly against taking the warnings literally. I believe in picking up the baby as much as possible.

To the infant who does not yet know any other means of self-expression, crying is the only way to draw attention to his needs. As long as he is crying, he is trying to ask for something, and to leave that appeal unanswered is to reject his earliest demand for vocal communication.

It has already been widely accepted as common sense that the infant's communication with the mother, particularly through touch—"skinship"—is important in the mental development of the child. An interesting experiment on this point was made by Dr. Harry Harlowe, head of the Primate Research Center at the University of Wisconsin, who had a newborn monkey baby taken away from its mother, offered it various artificially made mothers as substitutes, and studied what kind of mother the monkey baby sought.

One cylindrical substitute mother was made of wire, the other of cloth. Each doll was equipped with milk feeders and could be made to sway in a rocking motion. The result revealed that the monkey baby chose the warmth and soft touch of the cloth mother, and responded to the swaying motion. Dr. Harlowe concluded that the human baby too would tend to seek warmth, softness of touch, and rocking, and that the mother's gentle holding of the infant in her arms is as important for the emotional health of the child as her milk is for its physical well-being.

The reason I advocate holding the infant as often as possible is that I wish babies to have enough of this "touch" communication with their parents, as I see it as an essential part of the foundation of a sensitive human being. It is said that the famous wild boy of Aberon found his greatest security in having his hands held.

It Is a Good Thing for Parents to Take Their Babies into Bed with Them

Like the habit of holding the baby in the arms, sleeping with one's young child has also been condemned in Japan as an undesirable habit from the old days. Of course, it is troublesome if the child will go to sleep only if one of his parents lies down with him; but I have never heard of a case in which parents were completely at a loss in such a situation. On the contrary, it seems that new meanings can be found in this habit of sleeping with the small child, in terms of the healthy development of the child's ability and character.

One meaning is that the mother whose hands are full all day long and who hardly has enough time to communicate with her child has at least some time for such a purpose when she lies down with him and stays beside him until he falls asleep. Another point is that during that short time before the young child goes to sleep, his state of mind is very peaceful and readily receptive, so that if, instead of merely lying down with the child—or even falling sound asleep before the child does—the parent sings a song, tells a story, or reads a book, the impact on the child will be a very creative one.

It can also be suggested that instead of the mother, it is the father, after being absent all day, who should be the one to use this chance of communicating with the child. Dr. Seiji Kaya, formerly president of the

University of Tokyo, used to read a book to his child before he went to sleep, and he tells how, himself half asleep, he would read a book and begin to doze off, but if he stopped reading he would often find his child still awake and listening. Dr. Kaya remembers the experience with pleasure, but only years later was he reassured by the educationalists that that habit had been good.

It is also reported that research has been done in the Soviet Union on a method of learning in sleep. While still in a stage of light sleep before falling sound asleep, one listens to recorded information which remains in one's subconscious memory, ready for easy recall when it is reinforced in a state of wakefulness. This study is an indication that as yet unpredicted results may be obtained by offering learning experiences to the young child just before he falls asleep.

A Child Brought Up by a Tone-Deaf Mother Grows Up to Be Tone Deaf

"My child is tone deaf. I don't know what to do. There are many tone-deaf relatives on his father's side. So it must be a hereditary trait." I have often heard a mother complain in this way. True enough, there are tone-deaf children whose parents are tone deaf. However, this does *not* mean that tone deafness is a hereditary, or genetic, trait. On the other hand, tone deafness can be handed on from parents to children.

Suppose that the mother is tone deaf, and the child has to listen from morning till night to a lullaby sung out of tune. The child's mind will become accustomed to the mother's incorrect pitch exactly as it is, and using the pitch patterned after her model, he will sing songs out of tune in accordance with that pattern. Upon hearing the child sing, the mother will jump to the conclusion "My child is tone deaf—after all, musicality is inherited." Had Beethoven and Mozart been brought up by tone-deaf mothers, they would have been guaranteed to be tone deaf.

According to my theory, the tone-deaf child of a tone-deaf mother has a *superior* ability in hearing, for he can hear and receive exactly the incorrect pitch of the parent! Accordingly, I would imagine that both Beethoven and Mozart would have been *unsurpassedly* tone deaf.

Well, as an example to show that tone deafness is not a matter of heredity, I will give you a true story of a tone-deaf child cured of tone deafness. Dr. Shinichi Suzuki took on a six-year-old tone-deaf boy, living in Matsumoto, and cured him completely of tone deafness.

As is usual, this boy's mother was quite tone deaf. "A tone-deaf child is made so because he has been brought up by a tone-deaf parent," says Dr. Suzuki, whose technique was to have the boy listen repeatedly to the same song, in tune, that his mother sung for him out of tune. Dr. Suzuki said that the number of times that he had the boy listen to this song must have been four times as many as the several thousand times that his mother must have sung it for him. During that time, the mother's pitch pattern, formed in the boy's mind, was totally eradicated and the absolutely new and correct pitch pattern was formed, thus curing the boy completely of his tone deafness. This boy went on to learn to play the Brahms and Beethoven violin concertos correctly, and has since given solo performances in Canada.

Thus, musical sense in particular, and character and development of the brain in general, can be seen to be conditioned by the mother's daily habits. Her most seemingly insignificant and trivial behavior can immeasurably affect the small child.

Never Fail to Respond When Your Baby Cries

A recent American best seller by Maya Pines titled *Revolution in Learning: The Years From Birth to Six* describes the following experiment in infant education.

Specially trained persons were sent to private homes and children's institutions in Washington, D. C., to instruct small children. They were sent to impoverished districts, inhabited mainly by blacks, to visit some thirty babies aged fifteen months. Each of these special tutors spent one hour every day, with the exception of Sundays, with one of the thirty babies, playing with him and talking to him. A psychologist, Dr. Earl Shaefer, explained that his aim was to stimulate the baby's intellect, with a focus on verbal expression. In another, similar, experiment, Dr. Shaefer had nine young women visit homes to instruct fourteen-month-old babies.

The results of intelligence tests given to these babies at the age of twenty-seven months showed their IQ assessments to be higher by ten to fifteen points than those of control babies, especially in regard to verbal ability.

The experiments above were conducted to promote the education of babies born into poor homes where both parents had to go out to work. The success of these experiments in such homes as these should guarantee even greater success in more privileged homes, if parents take the trouble to play regularly and purposefully with their own children.

When a baby is two or three months old, he begins to laugh, babble, and remember all that happens around him. Before one knows it, he starts to carve his mother's trivial words and actions on his brain cells. Therefore, whether or not the mother is available as a companion greatly affects the development of the baby's intelligence.

Consider the following story. A young couple were living in a one-room apartment when their first boy was born. The apartment being small, the child and his mother were within earshot of each other regardless of what she was doing—and for her diversion she would be a companion to her baby when he babbled. But soon the family moved into a larger apartment with three rooms and a kitchen. Having extra rooms, the parents decided to have another child, and this time they had a baby girl. This child was reared in a quiet room away from the kitchen where the mother was always at work. Thus, whereas the older child started to talk coherently seven to eight months after birth, his younger sister was still only babbling at ten months. Moreover, in contrast to the vivacity of the brother, always beaming with smiles, the sister grew up to be very quiet and taciturn. It might be concluded that it was the degree to which the mother made herself available as companion to each of her children that accounted for this difference in their characters.

No Need to Talk Baby Talk to Your Baby

When I was dining the other day in a restaurant, I suddenly heard a little voice say from the next table, "Zhis time I say good-bye to you, Mum." Taken aback by this rather extraordinary statement, I looked round to see a boy of about two. In front of him was a dish of stew. Puzzled, I asked his mother for an explanation. "My child has memorized a television commercial for a certain brand of stew, and he must have remembered the lines when the stew was brought," she explained.

We adults are quick to forget the lines of television commercials shortly after seeing and hearing them; but the small child remembers them exactly, even long lines like this one, including the exact tone and intonation with which the lines are said.

People in most cultures often use so-called baby talk to infants and toddlers. However, television and radio programs are not conducted in baby talk for the purpose of communicating with infants, yet by the time the child is two years old, he can very well understand the language of an average program.

Of course, a baby only babbles when he starts talking. This is probably because of slowness in the development of his vocal organs rather than of his brain, so that his mouth does not move in coordination with his desire for speech. Therefore, if the grown-ups around him always talk to him in baby talk, on the basis of some prejudice that a baby understands only baby talk, correct language habits will never be connected up in his brain. To put it at its most extreme, the child may have to depend for the circuitry of correct English not on his own conversations with adults, but on listening to exchanges between the parents themselves and among other grown-ups around him.

It is not, therefore, necessary to talk baby talk at all. The young child is in any case expected to grow up to understand correct English within a matter of months; for once he is in kindergarten, the parents suddenly try to cure him of baby talk, saying, "You are no longer a baby, so you must speak correctly." This is imposing an unnecessary double burden on the child.

I have heard that a French mother on the occasion of her daughter's marriage will say to the husband-to-be, "My daughter is not bringing any dowry, but she speaks fine French." Such pride in a good command of one's language seems to me admirable, and I would like to see every child given the best possible chance to speak fine French or English or Japanese. And the best possible chance depends upon the experience from infancy of conversations in correct French or English or Japanese with adults. If we do not offer the children such opportunities, all of them will very soon have to be shouting, "Zhis time, let's say good-bye to baby talk."

Neglecting Your Small Child Is Worse Than Spoiling Him

There has been in recent years a growing awareness in the United States that the problem of black under-privilege, for some the most important concern the nation has to face, lies not only in race prejudice but in the upbringing of black children before school-ing. Many psychologists have conducted research in Harlem and various other black districts, and come to the conclusion that the differences in IQ ratings and character between black and white children are due in the first place to differences in environment before school age. Once they are in school, the differences in IQ formed in the early years are then compounded, and a widening racial gap between black and white becomes increasingly difficult to close.

Poverty, for instance, in many black families forces both parents to go out to work for a living, leaving the children virtually from the moment of birth to do their growing up "by themselves"—that is, supervised only by older siblings or casual baby-sitters. In contrast, the white children are likely to be brought up from the start surrounded by the earnest care and affection of the parents and others around them. This difference can be said to have created between black and white a problem to which there is no obvious solution.

Although I have made rather crude use of the topical contrast between white privilege and black deprivation, the same distinction might be made between homes in my own country, where contrasts in domestic environment are producing, for the same reasons, bright children and dull children, children with straightforward minds and children with distorted minds. We can, however, assume that these differences have stemmed not simply from differences in economic resources between parents, but also from differences in parental attitudes toward infant education.

One set of statistics (published in *Modern Esprit* magazine, No. 43) suggests that the more "permissive" a policy the parents adopt, the more insecure and defensive the children become. Such children seem to be hungry for love and tend constantly to seek the attention of grown-ups. Permissive practices as defined in the study included nursing the baby irregularly and feeding him only on demand, showering him with trivial toys, and neglecting to change diapers and underwear.

In contrast, although overprotection may produce a nervous and timid child, the infant reared in an atmosphere of profuse parental love and care is likely, in general, to be more able to adapt himself to society once grown up, and to be mentally stable and sensitive.

As more married women in our modern world go out to work, seeing themselves as no longer confined to housework and child-rearing, but as having individualities and definite roles in society, we also see more of the phenomenon of the so-called "latchkey child" who comes home to an empty apartment after school. I am not in any way opposed to a wife's cooperating with her husband to earn a living; but I am concerned that children not be neglected, or in the name of "permissiveness" be allowed to grow up without the adult love and protection they need.

A Young Child's Fears Are Often Rooted in Experiences the Adult Does Not Even Suspect

We like to regard early-childhood years as the happiest period in our lives, free of fears and worries about the complexities of life. However, in reality it is not likely that as small children we were always happy and buoyant. Just as we have worries in our sixties, toddlers too have their own insecurities and fears. And the reasons for these insecurities in the small child are often to be found in matters which to the adult are so trivial as to escape parental notice. An article in a magazine published by the Early Development Association recounts the following early-childhood experience of Mr. Shoutaro Miyamoto, head of the Kazan Astronomical Observatory of the University of Kyoto.

"My father must have been greatly interested in singing *Noh* songs. His friends often came to our home to practice. My mother busied herself serving tea and cakes, so I was left alone to go to sleep in another room. I remember being very much frightened by the oppressive and gloomy melodies of *Noh* songs, and crying aloud. But my mother was concerned about the comfort of the guests, and she tried to put me to sleep in a hurry. Even now it is terror that is roused in me, instead of a feeling of peace, when I hear that Buddhistic, gloomy tone." (*Early Development,* No. 4, 1961.)

Mr. Miyamoto's parents could never have dreamed that the *Noh* chanting would leave their son with such a fear, never to be wiped out even in adulthood. Mr. Miyamoto remembers with pleasure the stories of "Kizaemon Badger" and "Ikkyu Osho" that his grandmother told him before he went to sleep, and the sound of music from *Carmen,* and the *Moonlight Sonata* played on a player piano. Why, of all his early-childhood experiences, should the hearing of the *Noh* songs have roused such fears in him? It is something to give us, who are concerned with early development, food for thought: perhaps, for instance, it was not simply the oppressive, gloomy melody of the *Noh* songs, but the loneliness and darkness of the room where he was left by himself, that gave rise to the terror.

I do not mean, of course, to rush to a conclusion about what should be done in such a situation. I mean only to point out that what seems a trifle to grown-ups may leave an indelible scar in the heart of a child.

A Newborn Baby Senses Quarrels Between His Mother and Father

It is easy to tell at once from the infant's face that his parents do not get along very well: the infant's facial expression is one of gloom and anxiety. You might suppose that a newborn baby cannot possibly respond to the subtleties in a relationship between husband and wife; but a baby is endowed with a sensitive mind that reacts to every vibration around him.

What will happen to a baby who witnesses his parents' repeated ugly quarrels every day? Needless to say, he does not understand the significance of bickering between the parents, but he is sure to reflect in some way the feelings stirred up by expressions of hostility, which may come to inform his whole being. It is only natural that a child surrounded by anger and resentment has a dark and anxious face. It may be a matter of heredity whether the child has large eyes or a pointed nose, but the baby's facial expression is the very mirror in which is reflected the situation between his mother and father. I remember a marriage counselor describing being appalled, when a young woman came to seek advice about a divorce, by seeing exactly the same expression of sadness on her face and on that of the baby she held in her arms.

Such a child, in whom are implanted impressions of loathing and anger, will already, by the time he grows up and starts going to kindergarten and elementary school, have had his personality set in misery and destructiveness.

Any examination of the records of juvenile delinquency reveals that most youngsters in trouble have spent their crucially important early years in unhappy home situations. Their feelings and actions from the time they began to know what went on around them, and to act in social situations, have their roots in the unconscious experience of their early-childhood years before school age.

Dr. Shinichi Suzuki once said at a lecture, "When you go home today, line up your children. You will be able to read in their faces a history of the relationship between you as husband and wife." These words have never left me.

It is not particularly necessary to do any *special* thing to promote early development for your child. To create a harmonious relationship between husband and wife and a pleasant home atmosphere is the best start you can make.

Parents' Habitual Anxiety Is Catching

"My child is moody like his father" or "My child is careless like his mother," parents complain who are inclined to think that their children's virtues derive from themselves and their defects from the other parent. However, I hope that parents who have read this book up to this point have fully realized that what their children are, their virtues and their faults, are all the outcome of the way they have been brought up from birth.

Early development is often misunderstood as aimed at raising IQ ratings, or making toddlers read or write: things which can be measured by some means. But what is really much more significant is development of the skills of judgment and evaluation and of sensitivity, which are impossible to measure.

For these there is no particular program involved; it is how the parents act and behave and feel in daily life that is the very material on which the child is reared and which forms his mind and personality.

As I said earlier, a child born of a tone-deaf mother will be tone deaf if he listens to her sing every day. Likewise, a child reared by a moody person will be moody, and a child brought up by a careless person, careless. In the case of tone deafness, the mother who is aware of it can find a way not to affect her child by not singing herself but letting the child listen to tuneful records.

Nevertheless, one's character, emotions, and sensitivity are qualities one often does not discern in oneself. And even if one is aware of flaws in one's character, it is not easy to correct and improve them. Hence, it is essential to be extremely careful about them.

If the mother should catch a cold, she may well try to prevent her child from catching it too, by refraining from holding him too close or using an antiseptic gargle; in Japan, mothers often make the child wear a mask covering his nose and mouth. But there are not many mothers who try so hard not to give to their children their own character flaws.

The virus in a mother called "anxiety" is far more contagious and powerful than a cold.

The Father Should Communicate More Often with His Child

A child often grows to adulthood remembering with surprise the pleasant times he spent with his father, because these times were, in most families at least, so few. My eldest son has been and still is strongly impressed by the things we did together: rowing in a boat on the sea, and eating a dish of crushed ice with sweetened red beans on our way home from a walk. These events took place several decades ago and I myself have completely forgotten them.

The role of a father in a home has traditionally been the authoritarian role—he is the imposer of discipline, rather than the caring parent. If the child rarely sees the father except to be scolded by him, that child is likely to grow up rebellious, regarding his father as his enemy. An insecure child, because of his very sensitivity, frequently does not have good feelings toward his father. And though it may be that a child brought up by a very strict "education-papa" who outdoes his "education-mama" will turn out a genius or a hero, it is more than likely he will simply be submissive and lacking in character. And in the reverse case, where a father is a drunkard and brutal or obsequious to his wife, taking no interest in the education of the child, the child is likely to exhibit behavior problems and possibly become in time a juvenile delinquent. Such histories are common enough.

In most societies, I assume that the mother will have the major role in educating her child. But by this I do not mean that the father should leave this education entirely to the mother. To be a good partner to the mother—isn't this the father's role in the education at home? A harmonious atmosphere in a home cannot be achieved by the mother's efforts alone.

The other day I happened to be in a bus and observed a family of three who seemed to be on their way to a picnic somewhere. A little girl, around three years of age, was happily talking with her father.

Though not meaning to listen to them, I was beside them and overheard, "Papa, what can be made out of ten gums (chewing-gum)?" "Well, with ten gums you will have Guam Island. Wouldn't you like to go there with me?" (In Japanese, "gum" and "Guam" are pronounced alike, and the word for "ten" is pronounced like the word for "island," so the phrase is a pun in Japanese.) Thus they were carrying on a simple and innocent conversation. The mother was beside them reading a weekly magazine, as if pretending not to know what was being said between them. I felt that the father was positively trying to communicate with his daughter, and that the mother was taking care not to get in the way. This girl would grow up to be a wonderful woman, I thought. What sounded like a trivial enough conversation to a grown-up must have been a source of intense enjoyment to the child.

No wonderful child will be reared in a home where the mother is the leader in child care and the father only her follower, and no pressure for time or exhaustion after work should prevent fathers from having more contact with their children.

The More Brothers and Sisters There Are, the Better They Get On Together

The tendency in most modern countries is toward the nuclear family—a young couple living independently, separate from their parents and other relatives—and toward smaller families of one, two, or three children. Of course, problems of housing and employment have encouraged this tendency. Nevertheless, it has many drawbacks in terms of early development.

I was myself an only child, a circumstance at that time very rare. I was envious of my friends who had brothers and sisters and used virtually to push my way into my friends' homes, where the families had uproarious mealtimes and the children played and quarreled boisterously.

Interestingly enough, a firstborn in any home is often "the first born and least clever"; he is quiet and pleasing in manners but, to put it rather brutally, lacking in spirit. In contrast, one of my friends, the middle one of three brothers, was bold to a point of impudence and never cried easily, even when his older brother bullied him. He never surrendered even when both his older and his younger brother fought against him. I am not the only observer of such a situation; it is a common one.

Yet why is it that the children born of the same parents and brought up in the same home turn out so different in respect to character and ability? A generally accepted theory has been that the parents do not pamper their second and third children as much as their first child, so the second and third children develop naturally a sense of independence. But a recent theory on infant education has added another dimension to this hypothesis.

No matter how hard the parents try to create a good atmosphere in their home for their first child, and the stimulation and variety of experiences that he needs, he is at a disadvantage in comparison with the second, who has from birth the companionship and competition of another child to deal with and is thus likely to develop a far stronger and livelier character. Even more does this apply to the third and the fourth children, who will be trained to be tough and strong in both body and personality.

A child who takes violin lessons, for instance, and whose older brother or sister is also taking lessons is said to learn and improve very rapidly. Perhaps this is because this child has listened to his brother and sister perform at a concert and has been fired with ambition to do the same; perhaps he has been attracted to the records that they play. In any case, he has probably listened to them playing from the moment of his birth, and the sounds of their playing have served as lullabies.

It is often said that "The poor have the most children," as though it were the number of children that keeps them poor. But many men born in poor homes make something special of themselves, and this may well be accounted for by the fact that a child is likely to grow up to be superior in both character and ability if brought up in a scintillating home where the more brothers and sisters there are, the more stimulated each becomes.

The Presence of Grandparents Provides Good Stimulation

Where young couples live separately from their parents, older people tend to be ousted from their role in the education of young children, as well as from their other roles in life, and they are treated as a nuisance. This is a general trend in the industrialized world. It is sometimes said that old people make a pet of a small child, as of a cat, and encourage him to be self-centered and spoiled, so that the parents will not know what to do with him. This sort of thinking seems to be particularly prevalent among mothers who consider themselves modern and progressive. I know of a family of three living in a tiny one-room apartment, having left the grandparents' home simply because the parents feel they cannot bring up their child properly when the old people are around.

Is it necessary to go as far as that to achieve a nuclear family? It is a questionable step in relation to the upbringing of small children, whatever it may mean in other aspects of life. Of course there are still instances in Japan even today in which mother-in-law and sister-in-law torment the daughter-in-law out of the house, treating the firstborn as the treasure of the house and other family members as nothing. Such feudal attitudes still survive. But it is also true that a situation in which several generations are living together has great advantages. There is among old people a great store of cultivation, culture, and wisdom in which the young could share; and contact across the generations is in any case an emotionally enriching experience. Any tendency to spoil the child is more than compensated for by the affection, the telling of stories, and the reminiscences, all sources of stimulation and refreshment to the child.

The great Japanese scientist Dr. Seiji Kaya says that the people who influenced him most in his early-childhood years were his grandparents. Dr. Kaya's grandfather was head of a village near what is now Akikawa-cho in Kanagawa Prefecture. He is said to have been so strict that he had merely to walk toward the house and cough in order to frighten a crying child into silence. Yet this grandfather's strictness was rigorously governed by reason, not by sheer shortness of temper. Thus Dr. Kaya was never led astray, although he became temporarily rebellious. He grew up to be a man of spirit and resilience. In contrast to his grandfather, his grandmother was a calm woman who quietly did her weaving all year round. Perhaps it was from his grandmother that Dr. Kaya gained his own powers of concentration: when he weeded the garden, it seems, he was never satisfied until it was completely clear of weeds! And according to the psychologist Dr. Akira Tago, it is these powers of concentration that have made Dr. Kaya the man of character and the world-famous scholar he is today.

Contact Among Babies Should Be Greatly Encouraged

I have already made the point that the mother who is in contact with her baby through "skinship" from morning to night is giving him in the most enriching way the stimulation he needs. This affects the development not only of the infant's intelligence but of his sensitivity as well.

However, the baby would benefit most if, instead of having a single bond with the mother only, he also had constant physical contact with father, brothers and sisters, cousins, and other babies. Some mothers keep their baby in the house all day and night, but it is very important to take the child out of the house and let him be in touch with other babies. This is not only to promote the development of his intelligence, but to cultivate in him the qualities of cooperation, sociability, and leadership.

Dr. Harry Harlowe, in his research with primates, has experimented on social contact among baby monkeys and its effect on the development of intelligence and sociability.

In the first experiment, Dr. Harlowe placed a baby monkey in an isolation room—a cage completely covered by boards, inside which was placed only the nipple of a milk bottle. The aim was to see how the baby monkey would behave if it were kept alone in the cage for three months, then taken out and placed among a group of baby monkeys that had not been isolated. This monkey, though it was at a loss when first placed in the group, began to liven up within a week, and soon played with the other monkeys. The next experiment was made on a monkey baby that had been kept in isolation for six months, after which it was thrown into a group. This one did not play at all; it stooped and cowered in a corner, never joining the other baby monkeys. A third experiment on a baby monkey that had been in complete isolation for one year proved that it was utterly incapable of playing, even with other monkeys that had also been isolated. Finally, an ordinary, nonisolated monkey was put in a cage along with the ones that had been isolated, and this poor creature is said to have had a nervous breakdown out of sheer loneliness. The IQ ratings of the monkeys segregated for six months or more did not approach anywhere near those of the ordinary ones.

Having read of Dr. Harlowe's experiments, I felt fully justified in applying their results to human babies and drawing at least a tentative conclusion that a human baby deprived of contact with a variety of people will be seriously handicapped in development of both intelligence and character. Now, as distinct from the situation in the old days, people often have little to do with their neighbors, but I would like at least to see mothers of young children making the effort to get together with each other for the sake of the children.

Quarrels Develop the Child's Social Skills

It has often been said that man is basically a social animal, impelled by his instinct to live in a group, and that it is impossible for him to live apart from society. On the other hand, man is also motivated by the frontal lobes of his brain, which assert his own consciousness of self. Thus he must always seek a harmony between his social and his individual being. Unless a balance is established between these two, he is unable to adjust to society.

The achievement of this harmony in man depends very much on early upbringing. I for one think that this is possible only on the basis of a pattern of thinking established early which insists both on the individual right to be respected and on the collective responsibility to cooperate. Communication among young children is the grounding on which such a pattern can be built.

A toddler around two years of age begins to outgrow playing by himself and starts to play with other children. The child who has been asserting himself under the protection of his parents begins to learn for the first time to be cooperative in a group. It is to be expected that he may come home crying because he has not been able to have his way, but he has been learning how to live in a group, both while playing harmoniously with other children and while quarreling with them. Quarreling, far from being a purely negative experience, is particularly important, because it cultivates in the child gregariousness at the same time as individual initiative.

Quarrels between children can be classified into three types: those in which the child takes the initiative in provoking another child; those in which the child must stand up to a quarrel stirred up by another child; and those in which the child fights in retaliation.

These different types of quarrels are manifested at different ages; for example, at the age of two the child is likely to be only passively involved in a quarrel, whereas at the age of three he is increasingly the one who provokes. This may mean that the self in the child is being formed and expressed increasingly.

There are various causes for disputes among young children, such as fighting over a toy, slide, and swing, or verbal abuse. But there is no quarrel without cause. Any attempt to scold, and teach the infant that it is wrong to fight, without ascertaining the cause does nothing to promote a spirit of cooperation in him. In fact, it may be said to be an impertinence on the part of the parents to interfere with an argument between children; it is like picking a bud, destroying a growing instinct for group life.

Children have their own reasoning among themselves; they assert themselves and cooperate with one another in their own ways. Here, there is no room for adult reasoning. Judging children's quarrels from an adult viewpoint, and preaching to them that it is wrong to dispute with others or that a child who quarrels is bad, only produces an unsocial and angry child. Quarreling can be seen instead as the first lesson in group living.

Spanking Can Be Used Effectively Only While the Baby Is Too Young to Understand Its Significance

"A foolish king surrounded by blindly faithful ministers"—thus some ironic wit described the baby, with his parents the blindly faithful ministers, obeying every word of their child, who is nevertheless thought of as the foolish king because he has as yet no understanding.

No matter how foolish the king may be, however, while he is very small and sleeping quietly most of the day, he is no great trouble to his parents. However, around two or three years of age, that child may very well have turned out so self-centered as to be almost unmanageable. Then the parents seem to think for the first time that they should begin to discipline the child. So they scold and punish the child whenever he does something "wrong," suddenly changing their role from adoring courtiers to that of "devil-tamers." Nevertheless, "taming" or "training" at this late stage achieves very little.

The damage was done by the parents' conduct as "blindly faithful ministers" while the child was under a year old, little as they themselves may realize it. A child around two or three years old has developed his ego, his sense of self, and he is ready to rebel. He can no longer be obedient to his parents. The more the parents scold and punish him, the more rebellious and defensive he becomes, and the parents in turn get ever more hysterical. It is a vicious circle.

In order to avoid this, there is only one thing to do—to train and discipline the child *before* he is a year old, before he develops his ego. For example, the infant should be kept on regular schedules of feeding and diaper-changing from immediately after birth. Regular schedules will help discourage the child from eating casually between meals as he grows up, and so prevent him from getting too fat, and even from falling into the habit of bed-wetting which sometimes persists right up to school age.

The natural parental desire to "bring up a baby freely, at least in infancy" can thus turn out disastrously. The infant during the first year does not feel or understand strictness or physical punishment. In contrast, the child aged two and three feels spanking very painfully. That is why spoiling the infant at first, then shifting to a policy of strictness only incites rebellion in him. The result is the opposite of what the parents have intended. Spanking can be effectively employed *only* while the infant is too young to understand its meaning.

Anger and Jealousy in the Small Child Are Expressions of Frustration

The infant cannot express his feelings in words; that is all the more reason for the parent to handle the child sensitively by reading his face.

Speaking from the young child's point of view, I doubt that the child is often as well understood by his mother as she thinks he is. It is much more likely that, pressed by the need to do the laundry perhaps, she is tempted to dismiss the child's feeling too lightly, not troubling to find out the cause of his anger or distress.

Professor Toshio Yamashita, an expert in infant psychology at the Tokyo Kasei University, has listed the following six points as causes of anger in young children:

1) Poor physical condition caused by illness
2) Physical misery, caused by hunger or fatigue
3) Exceptional excitement after an unpleasant experience or a frightening incident
4) Lack of enough exercise, so that the child is charged with unreleased energy
5) Temper tantrums to satisfy some specific desire
6) The example of irritable parents

From this list, it would seem that the causes of anger in the small child are mostly to be found in his surroundings and in his upbringing. If one does not identify and remove the cause for anger, but scolds him unsparingly or lets him have his way with the idea of quickly getting rid of the troublesome child, one will only make him defiant or self-centered.

The parent may think that he or she knows and thoroughly understands the emotional state of the child; but from the child's standpoint, he obviously does not feel understood, for he is irritated and infuriated. The firmness the child needs in his parents can distinguish a reasonable demand from an unreasonable one, and lack of such intelligent firmness produces a poorly adjusted child.

Jealousy in the child is said to appear around one and a half years of age. Jealous behavior is bound to accompany the arrival of a new brother or sister, especially in a first child who up to this point has been the only child, with the parents completely to himself. The child may be jealous even of conversation between the parents themselves, and such feelings often lie behind apparently unreasoning misbehavior in small children.

Every show of temper in the small child, in short, has necessarily its cause, which is frequently frustration. If the parents ignore how the child feels, and only scold or praise him, the child is left unsatisfied. What the parents should aim to do is to remove the causes of frustration, instead of suppressing its expression.

Don't Make Fun of Your Child's Weakness in Front of Strangers

This may sound like an unnecessary piece of advice, but I know an editor in a publishing house who has a striking habit. When talking to people, he incessantly pinches his nose. This habit becomes ever more conspicuous as discussions get more serious, or if the tables turn against him: that is, whenever his nerves are strained. Although he knows that he does this and is embarrassed about it, once he is sufficiently engrossed in something he becomes totally oblivious and his hand once more wanders toward his nose.

According to his own account of the matter, his nostrils, when he was small, were unusually large for his face. As children normally do between the ages of two and three, he used to pick his nose while absorbed innocently in play. Then his parents would say, regardless of the presence of other people, "Don't do that, or your nostrils will get even larger." As his self-consciousness increased, he fell into the habit of pressing his nostrils with his fingers in order to make them smaller, and could not rid himself of it even after he entered school, and his friends used to tease him about it. This experience was so powerful that he began to feel generally inferior and grew up very timid.

When he told me this, though not meaning to offend him, I looked hard at his face and found that his nostrils were not large at all; they were if anything small, and did not by any means stand out in his face—though even if they had stood out, I could not understand the insensitivity of parents who would expose his weak point publicly. Fortunately, this man had a sympathetic grandmother who always comforted him, and he was able to grow up into an effective human being capable of performing his role in society. But he has never been able to free himself of his bad habit, as he told me jokingly. However, it might have turned out anything but a joke. This small incident could have crippled him in his social adjustment without his ever realizing why.

This sort of example is not so rare as one might expect: there are many parents who discuss their children's weaknesses and defects in the presence of strangers, thinking perhaps that the children do not understand. However trivial the defect may in fact be, one can never predict what harm it may do to the child at a vulnerable stage of his development to have it publicly exposed—a small child, after all, has no way of knowing what is trivial and what is not.

For instance, a child whose curly hair has often been ridiculed in front of strangers may grow up with the habit of leaving his hat behind wherever he goes. This may sound like a perverse reaction, since if he does not wear a hat, his curly hair is all the more noticeable; but self-consciousness can cast very complex shadows on a young child's mind, and Sigmund Freud himself has described many examples of this kind of reaction.

Better to Praise Than to Scold the Child

Of the two techniques, praising and scolding, it is the latter that often seems the more powerful in influencing the small child; but in the long run this is not necessarily true. Scolding can develop in a child the perverse tendency to defy. The point is that both praising and scolding should be done only with care.

For example, imagine a mother carrying a glass of juice to a table. Her toddler, already eager to imitate his mother, demands to do the same, but the mother jumps on him—"Don't do that!"—for fear he may spill the juice. This is a wrong approach, especially if, when the same child gets a little older, the mother nags at him, "Why don't you help me?" Even if what the child wants to do may be a little beyond him, it is better to praise him—"How grown up you are!"—then pour a little of the juice out of the glass if necessary, and let him carry it. Such consideration is important.

Dr. Suzuki told me a story about a visit he made to a violin school in a provincial town where one child was seen as a peculiarly intractable problem. He played his violin outrageously badly, and no one, it seems, could help him. Dr. Suzuki said to him, "Will you play the violin for me?" and the child played dutifully. True enough, it was a dreadful performance, but Dr. Suzuki praised him. "Fine, fine," he said, and then added, "I can play this part in this way. Do you think you can do the same?" "Yes, I can," the child responded, and he took his lesson like a lamb, making a real effort to cooperate. It seems he had been scolded in the past for his bad playing, but what he craved was encouragement. Dr. Suzuki believes that children are much more effectively handled by praise than by reproof.

Nevertheless, there naturally are times when it is necessary to scold; and then, instead of merely scolding the child for bad behavior, it is better to show him an alternative or to reason with him. If the child should start tearing up a newspaper that you have not yet finished reading, for instance, instead of merely slapping his hand and taking the paper away from him, you could give him another newspaper to play with. If this is not done, the child's very proper impulse to be active is suppressed, and at the same time the object of his interest is taken away, leaving him nowhere else to turn or nothing to do. If you cannot think of an alternative, it is at least essential to give the child a reason for the prohibition. He may not fully understand your reasoning, but he is likely to find in your attitude a feeling of conviction that he does understand.

Part IV

PRINCIPLES OF TRAINING

STIMULATION AND A SENSE OF ORDER

Arousing Interest Is the Best Motivation

Two- to three-year-old children come every day, led by their mothers, to Dr. Shinichi Suzuki's violin class, to take lessons. And many must at first go reluctantly. They look curiously here and there or jump up and down in the corridor, showing no interest in the violin. To attempt all of a sudden to make a toddler play the violin can only lead to tears, tantrums, and an intense reaction against the instrument, for the child at this stage is beginning to develop an ego and a sense of self.

At the beginning, therefore, Dr. Suzuki lets the child do what he wants when he comes every week, and he deliberately does not give him a violin. Very soon he finds that the child sits down quietly and watches a child of his own age playing. Within two or three months, he will have memorized the entire piece that his friend has been playing, and will himself be eager to play it. The teacher will wait for the point at which the child can no longer control his enthusiasm, and only then does he give him his first lesson on the violin. This period of waiting varies with different children, but at the longest it lasts about six months.

"Arousing interest is the best motivation" is the fundamental principle of Dr. Suzuki's teaching. In his view, forcing a reluctant infant to "study and practice" is the worst thing you can do. Once the child shows a real interest in the violin, he will make rapid and remarkable progress, sometimes even to Dr. Suzuki's surprise. As the proverb says, "What one likes one will do well," and there is no education method more effective than engaging a child's real interest and enthusiasm. For this, the parent's main role is in arousing that interest: instead of teaching the child how to count, the parent should interest him in numbers, and instead of teaching the writing of letters, interest him in writing itself. In other words, the parent's role is to prepare the child for education.

Of course, to arouse an interest, it is essential to create the right conditions for it: there is no way, for instance, of rousing a child's interest in drawing without providing him with crayons and paper. It is by having crayons and paper always around him that the child develops a desire to draw. Demanding that the child show an interest without paving the way for it is like commanding a dog to beg without offering him any food.

Many an adult who dislikes music or painting can bear witness to this, and can trace this dislike back either to once having been forced into taking lessons in these arts or, on the other hand, to never having had a chance to be familiar with them.

The Young Child Shows Interest in Whatever Has Rhythm

The record *Fox in Socks* is tremendously popular among American children, together with the picture-book of the same title, by Dr. Seuss. It is an educational record, an exercise in practice in language,

and as you can tell from the title, the *oks* sounds
form a rhyme. And the rhyming words in turn create
a rhythm. The record also has a lively melody and
a regular beat to which not only children but grown-
ups like me cannot help responding. This record is
meant not to coerce the children to learn the words
by heart, but to let them absorb them naturally
through the rhythm. And that is what has impressed
me most about it. It encourages a child to study language while enjoying the music, without any trace
of mechanical memorization or training. It may be
that much of the achievement in early education in
the United States is due to this emphasis on interesting, rather than compelling, the child.

Most of us are apt to respond negatively to the word
"study," as if preparing ourselves unconsciously to
refuse, suggesting that an association with the concept of compulsion has been deeply implanted in us.
Study should really be done with enjoyment. Just as
in the Japanese proverb that says "A shop-boy near
a temple learns to chant a sutra," the son of an acquaintance of mine, who is a monk in a temple, has
learned all of the sutra that his father chants every
morning. This sutra is rhythmical and is chanted
in time with a gong, so the boy must have learned
it naturally. Yet it would have been an agonizing experience to be forced to memorize it.

To Small Children, What Is Interesting Is Right and What Is Disagreeable, Wrong

Would you scold your toddler for tearing the wallpaper? How would you explain that what he was doing
was "wrong"? You distinguish "right" from "wrong"

on the basis of your experience, and of the morality of your society, but the child only a few years old has no way of telling whether it is right or wrong to tear wallpaper. If he is rebuked severely, he may not want to do it again, so as not to repeat the unpleasant experience of being scolded. But he may at the same time be quite crushed by the episode, which could have a lasting effect on his budding creativity.

Mr. Seishiro Aoki, a child psychologist, has been studying how the child tells right from wrong. He says that the child regards as "good" any experience which gives him a feeling of excitement or pleasure. For instance, abducted children whose cases have been headlined in the newspapers have been quoted, in response to parental interrogation afterward as to why they went off with a stranger, as replying, "He was interesting. He was not bad." It seems that kidnappers know their child psychology, and how to attract children by intriguing them! The small child, who regards as good whatever interests him, follows the abductor without suspicion.

This identification of what is "good" with what is pleasant and agreeable belongs only to the very early years. When the child becomes a little more experienced, he begins to equate the good not with what is pleasurable but with what is praiseworthy. If he does an errand and is praised for it by his mother, he concludes that what he did was good, or right. In contrast, he considers as bad, or wrong, what he is reproached or punished for, so that he feels resentful or miserable. He identifies what is wrong by its unpleasant results.

Let us suppose that you continually reproach your child for playing the violin badly, or for failing to learn to read. To the child, the whole experience will appear as something that makes him suffer, hence wrong, or bad: just as tearing the wallpaper is wrong, so is playing the violin. Some of us have grown up with a lifelong detestation of the violin or of a foreign language simply because our experiences of it in early childhood were unpleasant in this way.

Hence, instead of imposing your adult concept of right and wrong on your child, it would be far more effective to see that he has pleasurable associations with what is "good" and unpleasant ones with what is "bad." Your child will develop freely and rapidly any talent that he has, depending on how you allocate praise or blame.

Your Child's Interest Is Meaningful Only If Kept Up

Although I have said earlier that what is interesting to the child is the best stimulant, there is one problem involved here: it is extremely difficult for a toddler to keep his interest focused on a single activity, simply because of his infinite curiosity. If he is left to his own devices, he tends to shift his attention from one thing to another with a rapidity that his parents find quite bewildering. Up to a point, this is proper to his stage of development, and any attempt to force him to concentrate on any one thing can only frustrate him. His curiosity is necessary, opening him to a variety of experiences of the world, which are vital to the development of his mind and body.

However, I do not recommend that the child be left entirely to his own devices. Just as there is a problem for a child whose interest is restricted to only one thing—the most extreme form of which is autism—there is also a problem for a child who is incapable of concentration, in that he is in danger of growing up with a "butterfly mind."

The child does, normally, come naturally to find among the many stimulating things in the outside world an object of special interest which he cultivates all by himself. However, in most cases, some assistance in this process is necessary from parents. Whether or not the parents notice and react quickly as soon as their child shows signs of developing such a special interest is often of paramount importance to his sustaining it. As I have mentioned earlier, a budding interest can grow in a flash or just as quickly wither, so it is very important for the parents to catch precisely that moment. One can never know which of the child's interests has the possibility for growth and expansion, but at least he should be given the chance whenever the possibility is recognized.

A certain father, a consumer researcher, in Matsu-yama City, wrote me a letter reporting his own success in identifying a budding interest in his child at the right moment, and helping him to sustain it. According to his letter, the father noticed that at the age of a couple of months the child was for some reason fascinated by a letter of the Japanese alphabet, *no*. (In the Japanese alphabet, the sound *no* is written as a single letter.) The father proceeded to point out to his child any word that had the letter *no* in it: aji*no*moto (monosodium glutamate) and *no*ri (an edible seaweed) on the table, and asu *no* tenkiyoho (weather forecast for tomorrow) seen on television, each time pronouncing the word for him. Around the age of four months, this child memorized ABC, and so the father taught him XYZ, WTF, HNM, using an alphabet chart as a visual aid; the child memorized them quickly. At the age of eighteen months, he began to show an interest in trademarks of automobiles and electrical appliances, so the father encouraged him to point out and identify the trademark in response to his naming of a trade name; and, conversely, to name a trade name in answer to the trademark or brand name.

This effort on the part of the parent, though from one point of view simply a trivial exercise by a doting father, would be far from insignificant in maintaining and expanding the child's range of interest and experience.

"Repetition" Stimulates Interest Best

If an adult finds himself made to listen repeatedly to the same story, say three or four times a day, he is likely to grow very tired of it. Being impatient myself, I become irritated and restless if I have to listen to the same story even twice. Yet as a small child, I begged my father and mother to tell me the same fairy tales over and over again, without ever growing weary of them. It is very difficult, when I think about it now, to put myself in that small child's place.

Yet, as I have already said, repetition is of great importance to the circuit-connecting process that is taking place during early life to form the "hardware" of the brain. Repetition of the same thing, over and over, is desirable not because a baby never gets bored, but because infancy, being a period when children do not yet know boredom, is the time for developing correctly the circuitry system that is essential to future intellectual functioning. A three-month-old baby can memorize a complicated piece of music if he is made to listen to it several times a day, for the infant's capacity for absorption is remarkable indeed.

Repetition during the early years has another important function in stimulating interest in the child. As the young child memorizes fairy tales and songs which he has heard repeatedly, he begins to demand to be told or sung one particular story or one particular song, and to ask endless questions about it. He memorizes the tale of his choice, and at the same time expresses his curiosity about it and about the world.

And curiosity gives rise to interest, which gives birth to the will essential to the child's growth into adulthood. This will to act, to be effective, does not grow, as it were, on a blank piece of paper. Interest stimulates will, and this will alone motivates man to progress. Thus a baby who hears fairy tales over and over again grows up to be a toddler and begins to show an interest in a picture story, then in the letters of the alphabet, and is finally impelled to do the reading by himself.

Certain parents I know of, who were both working, put their newborn baby into a nursery for a year and two months. When the baby came home, his development was severely retarded. Yet around four or five years of age he began to take a great interest in music, particularly in lessons in violin and piano. The perplexed parents discovered that the child had indeed suffered from lack of stimulation in the nursery; but before going to bed and while doing exercises, he had been played records of Schubert and Mozart melodies and "The Skaters' Waltz." The lack of mental stimulation on the one hand, and repetition of certain pieces of music on the other, had led to near retardation in his intellectual development but a high degree of sensitivity to music. I feel that I have received a priceless lesson in early development from the story of this child.

Imagination and Fantasy in Young Children Are the Germs of Creativity

I have often heard parents say, "I want to bring up my child to be very creative," and I have written a lot about creativity in small children in this book. But I fear that present educational systems, in most parts of the world, emphasize only the cramming of knowledge into the child's head. Children are being educated to be well informed; but when they grow up they do not know what to do with themselves. This has led me to think of the necessity of fostering real creativity in children during their early years.

What is creativity? It is extremely difficult to define, but at the simplest level I take it to mean free expression of imagination and intuition, in the context of some serious concern; and at a more advanced level, some form of invention or discovery. At this high level of creativity, intellect, learning, and imagination function together. What is certain is that all such achievement has its starting point in the subjective emotional experience and receptivity of early childhood. This means that the child's dreams and fantasies, often seeming so irrelevant to adults, are the very germs of creativity.

Suppose, for example, you give your child a finger doll or an animal mask. He will identify himself with it and become that animal, perhaps making up his own story based on an actual experience at the zoo, or in a story he has been told. Similarly, his response to a painting may stretch his imagination in his own individual way, inconceivable to any grown-up. The great Renaissance painter and scientist Leonardo da Vinci is said in his earliest years to have seen witches hovering on the ceiling and strange-looking creatures stirring among the stains and in the cracks in the walls of his house.

Suppose that an adult draws a picture of a pot, and the child sees it as a fish with a big mouth, wide open. The grown-up may rebuke him, saying, "Don't be foolish. This is a pot, not a fish." But this response would be a mistake; it is like plucking the bud of imagination just when it is ready to blossom.

The following is a story by a five-year-old child published in the magazine *Early Development*. It is an illustration of the free, creative imagination of the child, which it is most important for parents to accept and encourage, never to crush.

A man tried to get hold of a basket and found in it gold pieces. And so he took them home, and then the gold pieces turned into leaves. Again, he found a basket under a cliff. He opened it a little bit and found in it many kinds of fruit. He ate them all, and then he went to a field and picked many flowers. That's all.

Cultivate the Intuition (Sixth Sense) in the Small Child, Rather Than Technique and Reason

Man is normally said to possess five senses: sight, hearing, smell, taste, and touch: but in addition he has another, the so-called "sixth sense." The sixth sense in woman is particularly good for detecting her husband's extramarital love affair; but, in truth, the sixth sense is an important element in anyone who accomplishes something great. We call a man whose sixth sense is highly developed "a man of strong intuition." Men who have made great inventions and discoveries have always relied on this sixth sense, no matter how many their years of study and research.

It can be said that because intuition transcends the five senses, it is the most ancient and fundamental of all the senses. Also called "animal instinct," it is beyond logical judgment and reason.

I have previously said that children up to the age of three are very close to being animals, and by this I mean that the young child who does not yet know how to think logically relies on his instinct. So it is important in early development not to lose sight of this factor, and to try to encourage the development of this instinct or intuition, rather than attempt to suppress it by teaching him techniques or convincing him by logical argument and reason.

Dr. Shinichi Suzuki tells a story in one of his books about the importance of cultivating the instinct. The case is admittedly an unusual one, because it is about Dr. Suzuki's experience in teaching a blind boy named Teiichi how to play the violin. Dr. Suzuki felt at first that it was impossible to teach a child who lived in utter darkness to play the violin, because of the highly delicate nature of the skill involved; the child could not even see what the violin looked like! However, once Teiichi was admitted into school, Dr. Suzuki did his very best to teach him, experimenting with a variety of methods and maintaining great patience. What Dr. Suzuki did first was train the child to hold the bow and to move it from left to right and up and down. Next he made him poke at the palm of his left hand with the tip of the bow, thus enabling him to "visualize" the bow in his mind's eye. At the start, the child had little control over the bow, but within two weeks he was hitting the right place two or three times out of five, and finally was able to point correctly even to the tip of his left thumb. Dr. Suzuki's great efforts bore fruit: one year later, Teiichi played Seitz's Violin Concerto—not at all easy to play—in Hibiya City Hall. This was indeed the triumph of an attempt to cultivate intuition: to enable the child to "feel" the position of the tip of the bow that he could not see.

Furthermore, insofar as intuition is a sum of the five senses, this training of the intuition will in turn tend to sharpen those five senses separately.

There Is Sex Distinction in Early Education

When a baby is born, the parents are likely to dream endlessly as to the future of the child: "Will he go into politics?" or "Will we have a lovely, gentle girl?" This parental love is far from being purely self-interested or egotistically ambitious; there is no harm in dreaming. But it is worth questioning the way in which we tend to see the newborn baby differently according to whether it is male or female.

In fact, children up to three years of age show very little gender distinction, in either mind or body. On many occasions we don't know whether to say, "What a sweet boy" or "What a lovely girl." As if to reflect this dilemma, many languages use the neuter pronoun "it" in reference to a baby, making no sex distinction. And the academic view supports this neutrality, suggesting that so-called "masculine" and "feminine" characteristics manifest themselves only after three. A well-known child psychologist, Van Orstein, for instance, concludes from his research that it is only after the age of three that the infant's behavior begins to reflect his sex, and that from the age of four or five boys and girls show real differences in the way in which they play, particularly with imitative toys. In a sense, the only sex distinction to be found in children before the age of three is in the mere shape of their genitals.

For all this, parents fuss over what is suitable for their newborn baby according to its sex. So the baby boy who does not yet know his own taste has to have blue clothes because to the parents, pink clothes would be improper.

But what is wrong with a boy's wearing pink clothes, or giving a girl a baseball bat and a toy truck? Must one deprive a boy of a doll when he happens to take an interest in one? Why say, "Don't you know you are a boy?" And who are we to disapprove just because a girl happens to like wrestling? The German poet Rilke was brought up like a girl, dressed in girl's clothes, but this does not at all mean that he grew up to be womanish. Instead of worrying about making a boy girlish or a girl boyish, shouldn't you be worrying about the harm you are doing in limiting your small child's special potential by your preconceived notion of sex distinction?

Don't Lie About Sex to Your Child Because of His Age

I have noted recently a great boom in magazine articles and television programs about "sex education," with the focus on when to begin to teach it, whether in elementary school or in high school. When you think about it, this emphasis is quite inappropriate. Why should sex, a matter of human instinct, be hidden from children up to a certain point, and then taught suddenly at school? It is unfair both to the one who has to teach it and to the ones who are taught to start discussing sex all of a sudden after it has been lied about and concealed while the children were toddlers.

For even a very young child, himself still close to being "neuter," starts to interest himself in differences between the sexes around two to three years of age. Discovering the physical differences between his parents, the child asks his father, perhaps while they are taking a bath together, "Daddy has a wee-wee; why doesn't Mommy?" Such a question is very natural. When a sister or brother arrives, the toddler comes up with the simple question "Where did the baby come from?"

When such questions arise, I hope that the parents are willing to answer them clearly; camouflaging the questions with a laugh, or lying, only leaves the child unsatisfied. The parent's embarrassment can only implant in the child the idea that one is not supposed to know about sex, thus redoubling his curiosity and at the same time distorting it.

The two- to three-year-old in particular intuitively sees through lies. He may pretend to be satisfied, but his curiosity has really been reinforced by suspicion at the parents' unusually odd behavior.

The argument that the toddler is too young to understand does not apply to the question of sex, either. It should be discussed directly in loving language, so that his first understanding of it is natural and accepting. If sex is not to be associated with darkness and obscurity, the adult must not lie about it. The reason adults so often cannot free themselves from the idea of sex as something shameful to be concealed is that they were not rightly educated about it when they were small.

Unbalanced Diet Leads to Unbalanced Eating Habits Through Life

Feeding problems arise in the upbringing of nearly every child. Books on child care and women's magazines are full of articles on "The Diet to Cure Unbalanced Eating Habits," or "How to Persuade Your Child to Eat the Foods He Dislikes." However, the approach of early development is to ask ourselves how to avoid the causes of unbalanced eating habits, rather than how to cure them.

Once a bad eating habit is developed, it is difficult to eradicate it. Dr. Masaaki Honda, a pediatrician and director of the Early Development Association in Tokyo, had the following experience. A man who was known to be very fond of oysters found himself served oysters meal after meal until he was heartily sick of them. Yet again a dish of oysters was offered to him. Controlling the nausea he soon began to feel, he made himself eat all of them out of consideration for the generosity of the person who had offered them to him, but the result was disastrous. He vomited, broke out in an eczema rash, and began to suffer from diarrhea. Eventually his constitution became so abnormally sensitive to oysters that he developed eczema whenever he ate them or even sipped oyster broth.

Although this is a case of an adult, there is every

chance that a child subjected to a similarly monotonous diet may have a similarly abnormal reaction. He consequently may develop a permanent repugnance for that food. So it is important to prevent the acquisition of unbalanced eating habits by avoiding their causes.

It is my own view that, restrictions in choice of foods because of allergies or other medical conditions aside, bad eating habits are caused by lack of a well-balanced diet in infancy. If day after day you serve your baby the same unvaried meals, he will naturally grow up to be narrow in his tastes and resist any foods other than the ones he is used to.

One's sense of taste is almost fully developed in the years between one and three, just as the other senses are, so it is inexcusable to prepare meals for toddlers with nutrition only in mind, as you do for dogs and horses. Your infant does not say like an adult, "This tastes good," or, "You are a good cook," but it is very important that he enjoy a wide variety of tastes nevertheless. I would rather see the child given a tasty meal, to develop the habit of balanced eating, and let the parents, if necessary, eat what is not so tasty. The most careful attention should be given to the seasoning and flavoring of children's food, to encourage them to enjoy as great a variety of tastes as possible.

Mr. Hiroshi Manabe's experience is an illustration of the importance of training the small child's taste in eating before the age of three. He tells how he taught all of his children, around the age of three, to distinguish between different kinds of *raamen* (Chinese noodles). They have all grown up with a talent for finding good *raamen* restaurants, not in terms of their reputation or prices, but in terms of really tasty *raamen.*

A Sense of Time in Early Childhood Comes from Having a Well-Regulated Daily Life

Unlike the days when my generation was growing up, the present is an era of television. Especially for the children of today, life without television is, for good or ill, inconceivable, and unless parents are thoroughly familiar with the programs and characters their child watches regularly, communication between them and their children can be quite difficult.

Television in particular plays the role of a clock for the baby who does not yet have any sense of time. He identifies a certain program with the time when his father goes to work, or the termination of a program with the time of his father's return, or the appearance of a certain personage on the screen with his bedtime. Thus, regularly repeated programs form a basis for the concept of time.

It is generally said that babies live only in the present and have no clear awareness of the concepts of past or future. The concepts of "before" and "after," "yesterday" and "tomorrow" are said to come to him around two and a half years of age, when he begins to talk. In other words, it is commonly agreed that the young child does not clearly know the concept of time until he understands speech and can speak himself. However, observation indicates that the baby does in fact grasp something of the complex concept of past, present, and future through a weekly cycle of television programs.

The strict regularity with which the television programs are presented is far more exact than that of domestic activities, such as eating breakfast in the morning and having dinner after the father comes home from work in the evening. And this regularity of television programming can be put to good use in relation to the infant's daily schedule. It is necessary to keep the baby on regular schedules, whether for breast-feeding or for serving meals, not merely to train him to be well mannered, but to implant in him the sense of time.

I have seen mothers trying to teach their small children how to tell time by the clock well before they can read or count numbers. The toddler does not understand the hands of the clock easily, because he cannot relate to them yet, so telling him to go to bed by pointing to the hands of the clock and saying "It's eight o'clock, time for you to go to bed" will not get you anywhere. The toddler goes to bed not because it is eight o'clock, but because it has become dark and he feels sleepy. Daily-life experiences conducted with regularity are the basis for the child's later understanding of the abstract concept of time. For the infant, regularized everyday activity is the clock itself.

News Broadcasts Are a Useful Means of Learning to Speak Correctly

I remember hearing one mother say that she had her two-year-old child listen to television and radio news programs to teach him correct speech.

You may jump to the conclusion that there is no point in having an infant listen to a news broadcast vocabulary that he can't understand. However, the point is not to make him understand the content of the news program, but to have him develop a learning pattern as he listens repeatedly to the right pronunciation, accent, and intonation of the language.

Bad grammar and pronunciation are of course the product of the environment in which one has been brought up, and childhood environment so thoroughly permeates the mind that, as I have said before, it is beyond one's awareness and cannot be eradicated once one has grown up. A grown-up with his own peculiar way of speech hands it down to his child, who in turn will hand down his speech characteristics to *his* child. As long as this is repeated, language, already corrupted, is subjected to further corruption. This is equally true for Japanese or English or for any other language.

Only if correct and proper language has been well established in a circuit of one's brain is it possible to avoid drowning in the flood of current slang, in phrases and vulgarities that overwhelm one through the mass media, for instance, and so be able to enjoy making use of them without destroying one's own command of the language.

It should therefore be very fruitful for the small child to listen often to an announcer who has been strictly trained in how to speak his language correctly.

It Is Desirable to Expose Young Children to TV Commercials

Television has long been disparaged as the box which makes "idiots of 100 million people" or as "commercial pollution." On the one hand, it seems television is publicly approved as a means of relaxation and entertainment for those who are tired from work, but on the other hand, it is no exaggeration to say that most of the programs, with the exception of news, cultural, and conventional educational broadcasts, are looked down upon as inimical to good education. And above all, parent-teacher associations and "education-mamas" most despise the commercials which take up so large a proportion of broadcasting hours.

However, I would like to urge people to reevaluate the commercials from a different perspective. Of course, I do not mean to suggest that, governed as they are by the harsh reality of capitalism, they are a source of reliable information about life. But any parents who have little children must have noticed how intently they watch commercials. And I would like you to consider why.

There are two main reasons why commercials are so appealing to small children: in the first place, commercials are constantly repeated; in the second, they are spoken in plain words, completely devoid of complicated and ambiguous expressions.

These two characteristics are peculiar not only to television commercials, but to radio and newspaper advertising as well. However, television commercials are especially powerful with very young children, needless to say, because of the medium's combination of visual and auditory effects.

This unique quality of television commercials appeals directly to the infant's pattern-cognitive faculty through repetition, simple image, and sound. *Sesame Street,* which I mentioned earlier, is said to have been modeled on television commercials—a considerable tribute to their effectiveness. Commercials are rigorously aimed to achieve their best effect within a very short time, ranging from five seconds to a couple of

minutes, and it is their very condensation that capti-
vates the young child. He sees, memorizes, and re-
peats words and images which could very well em-
barrass a grown-up person, but the content of the
message to that child is not the point. It is the process
of memorizing that cultivates his pattern-cognitive
faculty and so encourages his intellectual development. That is why I think we should reevaluate television commercials.

FORMING CHARACTER IN EARLY LIFE

Musical Harmony Is Best Learned in Early Childhood

We have seen in movie musicals scenes in which a group of fellow workers are enjoying themselves singing together. Sailors or cowboys, supposedly not trained in music, join in an improvised song, their voices harmonizing naturally. We Japanese cannot easily do this, even though we were all once trained in music at school and are able to read music. Our traditional Japanese music is monophonic rather than polyphonic and has no chords. In addition, music education in Japan has been centered from the beginning around monophonic melodies, reflecting an adult prejudice that the concept of a chord is too difficult for the young child, so that it is better to begin with monophonic melody.

However, it is perfectly possible to teach chords at the start—for example, *do-mi-sol* and *do-fa-la* chords—rather than individual notes as separate sounds. This would, in fact, make it easier for the child to understand the differences between the notes in their relation to one another: as I have said before, the young child quickly understands anything that in one way or another reveals a definite pattern. So the combination of one note with another makes it possible for the child to grasp intuitively a relation between the two, thus making it much easier to understand qualities of individual notes. Absolute pitch, impossible for adults to learn, can be fostered in small children if they are given the right musical experiences early on.

Violin Training Develops Powers of Concentration

A violin concert by a thousand children took place on United Nations Day at Expo 70 in Osaka, Japan. It was to begin at 11 A.M., but most of the children, including the three- and four-year-olds, were already assembled, standing in the cold square, before 8 A.M. to tune up and rehearse. It was so cold that the adults found it almost unbearable in the open air, so the children's steadfastness impressed me very much.

I do not mean that a very young child should be so precocious as to be unnaturally self-possessed. A child should be what he is, lively and curious. Nevertheless, being lively and being easily distracted are not the same thing. The latter is a most distressing trait in an adult, for anyone who is not able to concentrate on one thing ends up wasting a great deal of time and energy on every task.

In contrast, a child who has developed good powers of concentration will grow up with great advantages. It is often said that "children who are studying music are very well behaved," which may suggest to you that strict discipline is imposed on the children by their parents, or that the children are very solemn and dull, but the opposite is the truth. They behave well not because their parents are present, but because they seem to be able to concentrate on one object without much effort. Therefore, they can study far better and accomplish a great deal more in a given time than other children. This means, of course, that they have more time left for playing freely with other youngsters.

A follow-up survey among mothers of children who had been through the Suzuki violin course revealed that all the mothers agreed that their children had never struggled over studying for examinations, and that they did very well in school in spite of spending plenty of time playing with neighborhood children. A new image of an intelligent child seems to be emerging, full of vitality and quite unlike the bookish stereotype who is as pale and thin as a bean sprout.

There is a phrase in the *Analects of Confucius,* "in harmony with music," meaning that musical sound softens one's nature and naturally perfects one's whole character. Violin education, like any other musical education, requires repeated practice, which in turn cultivates powers of concentration. It naturally follows that music contributes a great deal to character formation.

Violin Education Helps to Develop Leadership in the Very Young

It has become evident that violin education, one typical method of early development, produces other results in addition to inculcating in the child powers of concentration. It helps to develop leadership qualities.

Leadership, the ability to guide a group, is considered to be a trait of the adult world, and its development is accordingly misjudged to take place in adulthood. However, the truth is that leadership begins to develop much earlier than we usually think. It has been said that one baby in a group of more than two babies always turns out to be a leader. According to Dr. Toshiro Yamashita's *Infant Psychology,* the child who is a potential leader is, first, never distracted in his thinking and doing even if there are other children around, and second, whether in play or in any other action, he is always creating new things, taking the lead in putting them into practice.

These are the same abilities, these powers of concentration and creativity, that are nurtured by violin education. It is thus perfectly natural that many children educated in Dr. Suzuki's violin class are vivacious, energetic leaders, rather than pale-looking geniuses. And these children will turn out to be the future leaders in society, which is and always will be seeking people with leadership qualities.

The best example of this is Mr. Kouji Toyoda, Dr. Suzuki's favorite pupil and now concertmaster of one of the most famous orchestras in the world, the Berlin Radio Symphony Orchestra. A concertmaster is the leader of all the members of the orchestra, a post that requires not only musical talent but also leadership qualities. Besides Mr. Toyoda, there are several other men from Dr. Suzuki's violin classes who have leading roles in world-renowned orchestras. They are young (all in their thirties) leading German or American musicians, whose languages, customs, and temperaments are all different.

Musical Education Affects Even the Infant's Face

There is another interesting and amazing side to musical education: it changes the infant's countenance.

That one's looks are determined by heredity, just like one's blood type and the color of one's eyes, is normally thought of as an undeniable fact proved by science.

However, as you know from experience, man's countenance is somewhat influenced by his personal history. Enlarging small eyes or making a flat nose pointed are possible only by means of plastic surgery, but one's looks and air may be changed considerably by everyday experience. This change is very apparent in a child who has listened to music or taken lessons in music. This topic was much discussed at a meeting of the Study Group of Mothers that was formed by the Early Development Association. When they had gathered for the first time with their newborn babies, all the babies were alike, like babies anywhere. However, within four months, several babies who were experimentally made to listen to Mozart's *Eine Kleine Nachtmusik* turned out to be markedly different in appearance from the other babies— their facial expressions and actions far livelier and their eyes far more radiant.

In a letter to me, Mr. Choken Maruo, a music critic, had the following interesting things to say on this subject.

I have had many experiences that demonstrate the great effectiveness of "sound." Any sensitive mother must have noticed great changes in babies' appearance since World War II. . . . The causes are: 1) the cultural level of mothers has risen; 2) nutrition has improved; 3) sound stimulation has been overwhelmingly increased. As it is impossible for a one-month-old baby to improve his level of culture by listening to everyday language alone, he must necessarily be stimulated by music from radio, TV and stereos. It is certain that he is listening to music.

Also, Mr. Maruo has said that in serving as a judge in musical competitions, he noticed that the facial expressions of the audience changed completely in accordance with the kinds of music performed from day to day. It is hard to say whether a particular kind of music changed the facial expressions of the audience or the audience with similar facial expressions liked the same music; nevertheless, Mr. Maruo has pointed out a very interesting phenomenon. Furthermore, he has adopted a method of "bathing in music"—that is, placing a person in a musical atmosphere, in the conviction that music makes one beautiful. Isn't there a thread of connection between this and the Confucian phrase "in harmony with music"?

Learning Verses by Heart Trains the Child's Memory

> The snow melting
>   Upon a tree, whence
>   Coos a turtledove.

> Oh, the little kitten
>   Paws lightly
>   A fallen autumnal leaf.

> Crawl and laugh, child,
>   Grown two years old
>   From this morning.

The above are translations of *haiku* (traditional Japanese short poems of five, seven and five syllables) that were written by the poet Issa Kobayashi in the latter part of the Edo Era. Experimental classes at the Infant School established by Talent Education are using such *haiku* as these for memory training.

The reasons *haiku* are chosen for this purpose is first that they are short, compact poems with a rhythm that makes them easy to memorize; second, that they accord with our general principle that "pieces to be memorized should nurture the child's spirit and should be beautiful, cultured, and worth remembering for a lifetime; and at the same time they must appeal to children."

First, children memorize one *haiku* by Issa every day, and they are told about the background story of the poem to rouse their interest. The next day, the children recite the *haiku* they have learned, and memorize a new one. Thus the child's memory is trained through learning by heart something he enjoys. A child who at first has difficulty in memorizing one *haiku* after hearing it repeated ten times learns it by heart after hearing it three or four times by the second term, and after only one hearing by the third term. I have been told that the children can memorize about 170 *haiku* by Issa within a year.

The important thing is reiteration. If a child forgets a verse he has learned, get him to recite it again. Children who have been trained in this manner, I am told, can memorize a complete one-hundred word story after hearing it four or five times.

Some readers may still be doubtful of the value of getting little children to memorize Issa's *haiku*. I too was at first rather doubtful about this emphasis on memory skill. However, at the Infant School the aim is not sheer memorization of the verse but the development of the child's intellect, his creativity and thinking ability. The *haiku* are used merely as an experimental tool for this training.

If the child should show interest, the *waka* (another short poem, of five, seven, five, seven, seven syllables) is just as good. Learning should be geared to the fact that the child's mind has the capacity to absorb and remember between one and two hundred *haiku*. This memory equipment will get rusty if not used, and the more it is used the more smoothly it will operate, at the same time expanding its capacity.

The child's ability to memorize should be trained in every possible way during the time of his life when he delights in repetition.

Small Children Should Be Exposed Only to the Very Best

In the past it was the practice of an antique dealer to let his apprentice deal at first only with the most authentic and valuable antique objects in his shop. The idea was that the apprentice, having been shown only real antiques from morning to night for about half a year, would develop by this means a keen eye to tell the real from the false. Probably the ability to distinguish the real thing was patterned into his brain, so that he could see instantly through the subtle differences between the real and the fake.

This method of training applies also to early development. As long as the authentic is patterned into the very young child's brain while it is still like a blank piece of paper, the distinctive qualities of the real will be circuited into it, and it will refuse to accept the fake even in adulthood. If the fake is patterned into the brain, on the other hand, the brain will not be receptive to the real. It is the same with a toddler who learns a specific accent: in adulthood he will not be able to change his speech characteristics.

It is not always easy, of course, to distinguish the real from the false. Parents must do this in accordance with their own evaluation; but it is reasonable at least to consider works that have been valued through the ages as wonderful music or art. There is no need to give your young child picture books with crudely drawn pictures just because you think he cannot understand more sophisticated art. If parents really think Matisse and Picasso valuable, they should show the paintings of these artists to their child without hesitation. If they feel that Beethoven and Mozart are exciting, they should let their child listen to them as much as possible.

Once the pattern is formed in the brain, the child will use it as a basis and gradually come to evaluate and choose music and painting for himself. One child may go for jazz, and another for pop songs, but that is a question of their own temperaments.

Mothers throughout the world tend to scold their children if they sing nothing but pop songs, saying, "Pop songs are vulgar; don't sing them or listen to them." But isn't it natural that they should be interested in pop songs, when they have more than likely been reared on them almost since birth? The patterning for pop songs has already been formed in their brains, so naturally they are incapable of choosing more complex music. After such behavior patterns have become set, it is too late to start educating the children in good music.

Music and painting are but two examples of aesthetic taste's depending on early conditioning. In anything, if a good basis is firmly established, the child will have an easier time later in life. Parental assistance should be offered before it is too late.

The Small Child's Imitations Are Great Creations

When I was little, there was a man in my neighborhood who stuttered. I used to imitate his stuttering, and my mother would scold me, saying, "Stuttering is contagious, so don't do it."

I think I was about three years old—just at the most imitative age, it seems.

C. M. Jones, author of many books on infant activity based on his own observations, advocates, in order to cure a young child of fear of dogs, placing him in the midst of a group of children who are free of that fear: the idea is that his fear of dogs will be removed by imitation of the children who are not afraid.

I have also heard a mother speak of her success in curing her child of fastidiousness about food by letting him always eat with other children of the same age, whom he would see greedily accepting any food that was offered them. Again, we often hear of a child usually lacking in appetite who has regained it after having a meal in a friend's home instead of his own. In such a case the mother might complain sadly, "My child doesn't like my cooking." But the success of getting the child to eat someone else's cooking is only a kind of imitation, not a question of "good-tasting" or "bad-tasting" food. The child ate eagerly simply because he was following the model of his friend's appetite.

Such urges to imitate appear in infants toward the end of the first year, and after the second, toddlers begin to mimic those around them consciously and deliberately. They imitate not only the children of their own age but also grown-ups and their elder brothers and sisters. John Milton wrote, "The childhood shows the man"; and accordingly, parents and others involved in bringing up young children need to watch their behavior especially carefully while they are going through this imitative stage. Children around three years of age are ready to copy another person's gestures, manner of speaking—everything. The reason my mother scolded me for imitating the man who stuttered was that she feared I might really stutter if I continued to mimic him.

In addition to the possible effects of mimicry on one's manner of speaking, the young child's tendency to imitate also has great influence on his emotional makeup: a child may become nervous after playing with a nervous child, or afraid of airplanes after playing with a child who has a fear of them.

The young child's imitations, however, are not mere mimicry; they are great creative acts. So you should not be too troubled about them or you might find yourself plucking a creative bud, which is quite the opposite of what you intended.

Excelling in One Thing Gives Confidence in Others

Lessons in violin, reading, or a foreign language are not meant to produce geniuses, or even specialists, in these respective fields, but mainly to influence the general development of the young child's intellect. No education is better than to offer the child lessons in as many different skills as possible, rather than training in any one particular field.

However, in another sense, training a child thoroughly in one field also has its great merit: "excelling in one thing gives confidence in others."

There is no end to the examples that prove this point. For instance, in Dr. Suzuki's violin course there was a three-year-old boy who was for some reason very timid and rather a crybaby. His manner of speaking was at first very awkward, especially his pronunciation, compared with that of other children, and he always clung to his mother's back, like a tortoiseshell on a tortoise. When a violin was given him, he did not even try to produce any sound with it; he just continued to cry loudly, exercising his vocal cords. Because of his manner of speech, he was apparently teased by the neighborhood children, who all happened to be very mischievous, and this made him cry more, and he was never included in the group. However, after one or two months of attending Dr. Suzuki's class, guided by Dr. Suzuki's ingenious teaching, this boy started playing the violin, and after six months he was able to perform completely free of his feeling of inferiority to other children. He developed an unusual talent for pizzicato playing, and after that he seems to have developed perfect self-confidence. It was the child who took the initiative to practice, to the surprise of his parents, and at the same time he grew livelier and more playful in other aspects of his daily life. He started pretending to be a conductor in front of older pupils, and at home played leader in a group of mischievous local children. In addition, his manner of speaking became quite normal.

This sort of example is not limited to children. In

my student days, there was a young man who was for some reason particularly fond of English, although he disliked all other subjects. Even in English he was at first a very poor student, but he studied it very hard, gradually increasing his vocabulary and finally becoming the best student in his subject. Then he started to challenge himself vigorously in other subjects, and eventually he achieved excellent results in all of them.

But though this can happen to a grown person, it is much more likely to be the case for young children, who are still relatively free of psychological worry. As long as he is able to gain self-confidence, a child will have enough material on which to grow and develop.

The Card Game of "Concentration" Develops the Small Child's Ability to Think

There is a card game, with which everyone must be familiar, called "Concentration." All the cards are at first turned upside down; then each player turns up two cards at a time and gains a point if the two cards have matching numbers or pictures; if they do not match, the cards are turned upside down again. It seems simple enough at first glance; however, anyone who has actually participated in this game will tell you that it is extremely difficult, and adults can easily be beaten by two- and three-year-olds. Just try this game once with your children. You will join in buoyantly enough, assuming that it requires no skill other than your memory; nevertheless, you will probably not find it easy to score. You may note that a card with the number two on it is the third card from your right and fourth from the top, and another card with the number two is the third one in the upper left corner, but as you wait for your turn, you will forget completely where these cards are. Finally, exasperated, you will turn up cards haphazardly, and your child will give you a scornful glance.

In contrast to your frantic attempt, your child will play this to his advantage by effortlessly taking one set of matching cards after another. It isn't that your adult memory is unusually inferior, or that your child's memory is extraordinary. If you observe carefully, you will notice that your child does not seem consciously to memorize where matching cards are. Instead, he seems to remember locations of matching cards not as separate points, but as a pattern. That is, every time he turns up two cards, he remembers their locations by linking two points. This is a typical example of the pattern-cognitive ability of the small child to which I keep referring. We adults, on the other hand, try to memorize locations of cards as separate points: where they are from the right or where they are from the bottom.

This power of pattern-cognition is one of the superior abilities of the young child which we adults cannot possibly imitate. The child can grasp instantly and accurately the unique characteristics of any pattern. When you think about it, no memory skill is more efficient and dependable than this one.

The young child can develop this special skill through playing games, and also through music. In this, parents can offer only indirect assistance; but the seemingly trivial acts of playing with children, listening to songs together, and painting along with them actually contribute a great deal to their future growth.

CREATIVITY AND SKILLS

Give Pencils and Crayons to Your Baby as Soon as Possible

Around eight months after birth, a baby can hold an object in his hand quite freely, as he can now separate his thumb from his fingers. The ability to hold and grasp things freely, although it may not seem so significant at first sight, should tell us more than anything else about the healthy development of the baby's mind. Such activities as tearing books and papers and ransacking the toy box, which drive the mother to her wit's end, begin at about the same time. In other words, the child is approaching the stage of expressing himself.

It is most important, then, that the mother cleverly nurture her baby's will to do things that rises from deep within, for she will be paving the way to fostering creativity in the child.

Give your baby a pencil or some crayons. He will be sure to scribble wildly everywhere, and if you give him a piece of paper, he will draw lines furiously or tear it apart. But even a simple line, quite insignificant to us, is to him a means of self-expression.

However, most parents unwittingly suppress this very desire for self-expression in their children. They impose on the child their own ready-made ideas: "Hold a crayon like this"; "Apples are red"; "Draw a circle in this way"; or "Don't tear the book"; "Don't throw papers around"; "Don't write on the table." Is that not a volley of don'ts to pour on the child?

We often visit a home that is immaculately kept, with not a single scrap of paper lying around, even though there is an infant about. In such a case, the world pays compliments to the mother, praising her for being able to keep her house tidy and in good order while looking after a small baby. Indeed, it must be very hard for any mother to keep the house neat and clean in addition to caring for her infant from morning till night. But it would be a terrible blow to her if she knew that her diligence in house-keeping might be impeding the child's desire to create.

It is said that activities done with the fingers—such as scribbling, turning the toy box upside down, and tearing a piece of paper—develop the baby's intellect and enrich his creative ability. It is evident, then, that the sooner you give him pencils and crayons the better will be the result.

However, telling your baby not to do this or that, restricting him after giving him crayons and pencils, will only negate the gift, once again nipping his creativity in the bud.

Standard-Size Drawing Paper Produces Only Standard-Size Men

I met Mr. Hiroshi Manabe through one of the series of interviews published in the magazine *Early Development* by the Early Development Association. Like us, he was very much dissatisfied with current education for small children, and he has publicly made some remarks and proposals that seem to me to hit the right target. I would like to quote some of his remarks about painting, which is in his line of business as an illustrator, and about how parents could introduce this activity to their young children.

He says that the first decision to be made about a painting is, how large is it to be? Yet parents and nursery-school and kindergarten teachers tend to give children pieces of drawing paper all cut to the same size, thus taking that decision away from them.

This attitude is comparable with the adult prejudice, that only so-called children's songs and children's stories are good for children. It is an unimaginative limitation which in turn restricts imagination. Children who are given only standard-size drawing paper grow up unconsciously assuming that painting means only pictures of a certain size, and enslaved to the ready-made idea that drawing only miniature pictures in the small world of the standard paper will please their parents and gain compliments from their teachers.

There spreads out a wide, wide world in the child's imagination, far beyond parents' understanding, when the child for the first time holds crayons and pencils in his hands and discovers their traces on the pure white paper as he moves his fingers. That wide world is infinitely larger than standard-size paper, and I would like to see that child provided with drawing paper so large that he can draw on it while crawling. Standard-size drawing paper gives birth only to a standard-size man. And such a man will have neither the creativity nor the vitality to assume the responsibilities of the coming generation.

Too Many Toys Produce Scatterbrained Children

It is my opinion that many parents give just a few too many toys to their children. I have often seen a child in a toy shop crying himself into hysteria to get a toy he wants, until his parent is finally forced into buying it, his patience worn out; but many child experts believe that to refrain from giving the child everything he wants is not to lack parental love but, on the contrary, is in the best interests of the child.

I have myself often whimsically bought toys for my grandson in order to please him, and been rebuked by his mother. It may sound ridiculous to be scolded for buying toys for my grandson, but I have been made to reconsider my conduct after looking into the matter more seriously.

According to many psychologists, children with too many toys tend to be so overwhelmed by the choice of playthings that they are incapable of concentrating on one, directing their bewildered attention from one object to another. A child can play quite well with only one toy, devising his own diverse ways of playing with it; and for this imaginative play even a piece of wood or a broken kettle lid may be more interesting to him than an expensive toy sold in a department store.

If, then, it is the aim of parents to help develop originality and ingenuity in their child, to give him everything he wants will have the opposite effect. As in the Japanese saying "He who drinks drowns in the drink," I cannot help feeling that a child with too many toys is in danger of being overwhelmed by the toys.

It Is Not a Good Idea to Tidy Everything "Dangerous" Away

I was struck by a passage in a book written by the wife of Ango Sakaguchi, the well-known Japanese author. Mrs. Sakaguchi writes that Ango keeps his study so topsy-turvy that there is not even room to put a foot in it, and that if she (Mrs. Sakaguchi) is so unwise as to tidy the room, she receives a scolding from her ungrateful husband.

Ango Sakaguchi is not the only artist engaged in creative work who keeps his work space as untidy as a junk shop. And in my opinion this fact is by no means unrelated to their rich, creative activities. Whatever meets their eyes and whatever catches their ears no doubt stimulates the imagination and can be used as a source of inspiration.

The reason I mention this is that many mothers, oversolicitous of their children, tenderly put everything they feel might be harmful out of their reach. Babies, from the moment they begin to crawl or toddle, are so unsteady in everything they do that one cannot watch them without feeling nervous: they overturn vases, chew electric cords, or fall on concrete floors. It is understandable that mothers, not being able to bear the thought of any harm's befalling their children, do their best to protect them by keeping them away from every possible danger. But the logical conclusion of this would be to empty the baby's surroundings of everything but blunt and solid objects that do not break easily, leaving him, as it were, in a virtual vacuum.

I fully endorse Madame Montessori's insistence on the importance of tactile experience in infancy. She recommends that children be consciously offered coarse and fine materials, soft and hard, and blunt and sharp or heavy and light objects, to stimulate tactile imagination. A baby is fascinated by whatever surrounds him, and if he touches and fingers things with interest, and sometimes overturns them or tears them apart, it is only evidence of his expanding curiosity and creativity.

Just as an untidy work space may give inspiration to an artist, what seems to the adult to be trifling or full of danger may appeal to the baby's imagination, develop his intellect, and heighten his creativity. We should thus think twice about overprotecting or unnecessarily restricting children. However chaotic your sitting room, or however loudly the baby may scream when he hits his head on the vase he has just capsized, the chances are the experiences are precious ones for the baby!

The Infant Has His Own Sense of Order

Although it is not in the best interests of the child to keep a room too tidy, I do not mean, of course, to approve of slovenly households strewn with things that have been used and not put away. The infant's superior pattern-cognitive ability makes him extra sensitive to pattern, color, and location in space. And as his pattern-cognitive faculty is developed with constant repetition, I deduce that when he always finds a certain thing in a certain place he is stimulated in the same way as he is by the repetition of other experiences.

Madame Montessori and Professor Piaget have each quoted examples of this response to order by infants. One five-month-old baby, out of his carriage, showed particular delight at the sight of a slab of white marble mounted in a yellow wall. After that, he was taken there every day, and very soon his eyes began to sparkle whenever he saw it. Another baby showed his displeasure when a red umbrella was placed suddenly on a desk with which he was familiar; yet another fell into a state of excitement when given a bath held in his mother's left arm, instead of her right arm as was customary; and a fourth burst into tears upon seeing a cushion placed differently on a chair. All these incidents reveal how sensitive the infant is to any changes in his surroundings.

If you think about it, you will realize that similar occurrences arise quite frequently. A baby starts crying without any apparent reason, loses his appetite, develops a fever: all these may be his reactions to changes in his environment which are quite undiscernible to the adult.

In other words, any change in his surroundings means to the infant a disruption of his own sense of order. If that change is, in the eyes of the infant, a change from the pleasant to the unpleasant, he cannot help reacting to it.

What we have to realize is that infants are in fact far more sensitive to order than we adults are. The infant is not aware of only one thing; he grasps intuitively the relation between one thing and another, and this has much to do with the development of all his abilities. Thus, should we adults not carefully avoid disrupting this sense of order by our own insensitive, heartless treatment?

Give Your Baby a Place for Viewing, Rather Than Things to Look At

A peculiar thought has often occurred to me when I have looked into a crib and seen a baby's face: placed in the crib and not yet able to move his head freely, what is the baby staring at? Because of the limited range of his vision, what the baby who is laid on his back can gaze upon is nothing but the ceiling or a mosquito net. Sometimes an adult face appears out of the blue and then disappears.

This is not good. We must give our baby something to look at. Parents throughout the world hang mobiles from the ceiling or rattles from the side of the crib. But I wonder if this is enough.

My concern happens to coincide with that expressed in a book by Madame Montessori. She declares that the infant of this age is hungry for sensory stimulation, and that this hunger can never be satisfied as long as he is left lying on his back in a crib or carriage. Furthermore, although grown-ups may occasionally lean over him and break the baby's isolation, this adult behavior really puts a great deal of strain upon the baby's eyes. It is natural that babies, simply because they are so hungry for stimulation, will struggle to follow anything that catches their eye, but it is not a good thing to take advantage of this weakness.

One solution to this problem is to raise the baby's head a little bit by propping him up. Instead of constantly sticking your head over the edge of the crib, or offering him toys, it is far more important to prop the baby up in a position from which he can see the world outside his crib for himself.

Toys Should Be Interesting to Touch As Well As Pretty to Look At

Hiroshi Manabe, the illustrator, applies his ideas about early education to his own children, and he told me the following:

"I never buy a toy for my children that is ready-made. I give them only sets of toys whose pieces must be assembled before they can be played with. The children try to construct them, and even if the tears are running down their cheeks, they know that they are responsible for putting them together and therefore cannot ask for help from their parents. They know that unless they can fit the pieces together, they cannot play with the toy, so they work very hard."

I think this is an excellent theory of early-childhood education. Here is the "joy of accomplishment," which is so lacking if the child receives nothing but ready-made products. But it is very important that the toy to be assembled be appropriate to the child's age and ability, or Mr. Manabe's policy can become very cruel and very frustrating for young children.

In practically every toy store there are sensational toys, colorfully painted in primary colors: talking fairy-tale books like a picture-story show, toys with alphabet keys like a typewriter, decorative or instructive toys—all sorts. Even to adults, these toys are delightful to look at, taking us to a dreamland. We get absorbed in them unknowingly and empty our purses to the last penny, thinking that our children will be mad with joy to receive them. But the truth is that the children will play with them for a few minutes, and then may never look at them again. Every parent must have had an experience like this.

Children are not usually satisfied with a finished toy which is too little related to their world of immediate experience. For children, a toy must be more than nice to look at, and more than something that moves. Even with an expensive electric-train set the toddler may spend more time putting the rails together and breaking them apart than watching the train move.

The Montessori school of education is said, on the other hand, to have invented toys modeled on daily-life tools that the child sees used around him. These include coarse and smooth objects for feeling and throwing, objects for placing inside one another, and toys that require simple skills such as buttoning and unbuttoning or fitting on a lid. All these are closely related to the everyday activities of the child.

Adults often have preconceived ideas about toys based on our own childhood fantasies. The young child takes an interest in the things around him and responds especially to what gives him "the joy of accomplishment" and satisfies and fosters his desire to create.

To the Small Child, Books Are Not Necessarily for Reading, nor Building Blocks for Building

We adults unimaginatively assume that a book is meant to be read and building blocks to be built into something. However, to the young child a book is not necessarily for reading and building blocks are not necessarily for piling on top of one another.

Books and building blocks usually being the first things on the list, adults tend to impose on the children their own ideas of how to play with them. They are tempted thus to control their children's play activities. But if the children enjoy playing with the toys in their own way, the objective of playing is achieved, regardless of how or with what toys. To control the children in their playing again means nipping their creativity in the bud and even perhaps depriving them of the very desire to play.

Books may sometimes be used to make a tunnel, sometimes used as drawing paper, and sometimes utilized as something to tear apart. Insisting that a child use books for reading, which is a one-sided adult notion, might produce effects worse than not giving him any books at all! The small child will gradually find out for himself that books are most interesting when read when he takes an interest in reading itself.

No toy is more boring to children than a toy that is already complete and can be played with in only one way. No matter how expensive a toy may be, it is of no value to the young child unless he can use his hands to operate it and his inventive mind to adapt it to his own creative purposes.

Almost every parent must have had the experience of buying too many toys for his first child; most parents buy fewer for their second, having realized then that children do not particularly need many toys, but rather need a few very good ones. To the infant, whatever catches his eye and whatever touches his hands is a toy. There is no particular need to give him ready-made toys, or to insist that he play according to ready-made adult ideas of play.

Such Simple Activities as Clay Modeling, Paper Cutting and Paper Folding Foster Small Children's Creativity

I have been advising parents to avoid toys that are complete in themselves, and to give toys that are interesting to handle, rather than merely pretty to look at. What, then, are the most suitable toys which fulfill these qualifications?

If we look around, we may be surprised to be made aware once again of the value of the simple toys that have been used for generations, instead of newly created toys that are being sold for the first time. Among these ancient playthings are clay, paper for cutting, and colored paper for folding.

These materials all share a common characteristic: they are all devoid of concrete shape and meaning. In other words, these can take any form, depending on what one makes of them. This is the very reason they are such excellent toys for the small child at a time when his intellect is developing fastest, because they can be used in different ways as he develops.

Let us suppose, for example, that we give clay and colored paper to a baby under a year old. He will toy vaguely with them—not particularly meaning to *make* anything, but examining and observing them; yet even if he has no intention of manipulating the materials, the clay and the colored paper are changed as he handles them, assuming different shapes and forms. He observes the changes with surprise, and this in itself is an important growth experience.

At this stage, the infant will merely repeat the "toying operation"—on the one hand, interested in the changes in the materials, and on the other, pleasantly stimulated by the experience of touching clay or paper. And he learns intuitively the causal relationship between the action of moving his fingers and the transformation of the clay and paper.

Gradually, however, not satisfied with merely squashing clay or crumpling and tearing paper, the baby will begin to flatten a lump of clay and make it round, as if it were a plate, or to fold a little corner of colored paper as if it were a boat. Toys of this type are flexible materials out of which very simple things as well as very complicated things can be made, depending on different phases of growth.

There is a marked difference between the skill with which a child who has been introduced to clay in very early life makes things and that of a child who has not. This is not so much a question of familiarity with or taste for clay, but much more importantly is due to the degree of intellectual and creative development which playing with clay early has already stimulated. Dexterity and self-expression are only two of the qualities that such activities have nurtured in the child.

"Acting a Play" Develops Creativity in the Young Child

I have talked about my own ideas of play and toys in the preceding section. And just as the real purpose of violin education or language lessons is not to train the child to acquire a skill, but to bring out the infinite potential in the child, unstructured play is aimed at developing the child, not at achieving a predetermined result.

The Illingworths, coauthors of *Some Aspects of the Early Life of Unusual Men and Women,* draw the following conclusion: every infant, whether destined for "greatness" or not, deserves sympathy, encouragement, and help in order to develop the best in him, regardless of the class into which he is born or the color of his skin. We adults have the duty to provide this sympathy, encouragement, and help for our children, and this means, above all, time and patience with them.

Mr. Goro Maki, writer of children's stories, believes that drama is one of the best means of enlivening the young child's active creativity. However, he adds sadly, "playacting takes a long time to demonstrate its benefit to the child, so parents who expect immediate effects—'education-mamas' in the bad sense of the word—tend to be too impatient." According to research I have seen, children who have been encouraged to play at theater, to invent their own drama, do no better than other children, or sometimes even a little below the average, in the first and second grades in primary school; but in the third grade they suddenly begin to stand out, leaving other children way behind.

Let me explain here briefly what I mean by "playacting," or drama. This is not to be misunderstood as "pretending to be a character in a drama," nor is it exactly mimicry: it is a creative activity in which the child expresses actively what he himself feels and thinks through his body, instead of through an instrument or crayons. It has also nothing to do with speech training or recitation in public; though I do not mean to deny that a child who has had experience of drama in early life may turn out to have a splendid talent for acting or reciting in public.

The most important thing, however, is that it enables the child to express himself directly, and in relation to others in the group.

"Play" should always be basically freedom of self-expression.

Physical Exercise Stimulates Development of Intellect

When I have come back home after being abroad, I have often been struck by the feeble way in which Japanese people walk. According to Assistant Professor Kunio Akutsu of Tokyo University of Education, who has been doing research work for the Early Development Association, this slack walking posture is due to the lack of proper training in basic motor skills such as standing up and sitting down during infancy, when the nerve circuit begins developing.

Babies start walking eight months after birth at the earliest. Unless they are trained properly then in basic movements, they will never learn to do them correctly, or to acquire the more complex physical and intellectual skills based upon the same brain circuits. In this sense, the principle of early training in "walking"—in itself a very ordinary activity—is exactly the same as that of early violin education and foreign-language lessons.

I am going to discuss a baby's physical exercises in the next few sections because I want parents to be aware, first, of the fact that the fundamental motor skills must be taught during infancy, before it is too late; and second, that this training, if it is done correctly, greatly stimulates the development of the infant's intellect. There is a Japanese saying that "A superior mind dwells in an active body."

An infant's mind does not grow independently of his body, but develops in close connection with every physical activity and sensory experience. As I mentioned earlier, swimming during the baby's first year not only promotes the development of the infant's muscles but also sharpens the reflexes. And Professor

Akutsu says, "Giving a baby physical exercise improves the individual organs and systems of his body and strengthens and invigorates his resistance to pressures and stresses from outside."

Any baby left alone will grow, as long as he is given milk and protection; however, if this is all he is given, the full range of potential that he is born with will not be developed. Physical exercise is one of the first things he needs, because it stimulates the development of muscles, bones, and internal organs as well as the development of the brain.

It has been said that a child who begins to walk early is intelligent. And it may indeed be that he is that much more intellectually developed because he is engaged in just that much more activity.

Train the Left Hand As Well As the Right Hand

How many left-handed persons do you notice in your own immediate circle? One or two at the most? And even fewer ambidextrous people—in fact, hardly any. I don't know whether Adam and Eve were right-handed, but right-handedness seems at some point in history to have been accepted as the norm. Driver's controls in automobiles, sports equipment, and kitchen and craft tools are all made for the right-handed. So parents have traditionally tried to teach their children to use their right hands.

In America there seem to be many more "southpaws" than in Japan, but generally there are more right-handed persons than left-handed. But are there any valid reasons for right-handedness?

There is a strange theory that left-handedness puts

pressure on the heart, but I have never heard of a correlation between left-handedness and heart disease. But I do know the case of the left-handed man who as a child trained himself to use his right hand as well, and now has the great convenience of being able to use both his hands. When writing, for instance, he first uses his right hand, shifting easily and freely to his left when his right is tired. When I heard this, I tried in vain to train my own left hand. But at my age I find that my left-handed writing looks like earthworms crawling one on top of another. I cannot even aim a ball accurately with my left.

The right hand and the left hand have lived through the same length of time, and the bone structure of one is no different from that of the other. Why, then, should there be so much difference between the two? There seems to be only one reason: the two hands have been treated differently in infancy. That a southpaw's right hand is just as clumsy and awkward as the left hand of a right-handed man suggests that unless both hands were trained properly, they would not function at all and even picking up chopsticks would be impossible.

According to Dr. Shinichi Suzuki, monkeys are ambidextrous. Although they are supposed to be inferior in intelligence to the human being, they can freely use their two hands for eating and doing exercises. Human beings are thus inferior to monkeys in their use of the left hand. Again, I have heard it suggested that the right hand of a human baby could be partially incapacitated if the mother should happen to fall into the habit of breast-feeding her baby holding him only in her left hand—perhaps while using her right hand for something else at the same time—because the baby's right hand would then always be pressed against her body, and he would be forced to start grasping things in his left hand. Or it may simply be that if a child begins writing with his left hand, it begins to develop more than his right.

It seems quite possible, then, that one can develop ambidexterity. But this depends on training in infancy. I mentioned earlier that training in finger manipulation contributes a great deal to the development of intellect. From this point of view too, it is a pity to neglect the training of the left hand.

Small Children Should Do a Great Deal of Walking

Owing no doubt to the dangers of modern road traffic, we no longer see little children toddling in the streets, and when we do, they are likely to be being dragged along by the mother, rather than toddling by themselves. Before you complain that you don't have time to move at the pace of a toddling child, I would like you to think seriously about what "walking" means to the baby.

Walking is an exercise that involves the whole body: of the total 639 muscles in the human body, 400 are said to be used in walking. Unlike most other muscular activities, walking is not a continuous exercise, but a rhythm of "moving" and "resting." The correct way of walking always has the muscles of one leg moving while those of the other are resting. Thus it is a smooth motion with no waste of labor involved.

It is no accident, for instance, that writers often say that if they take a walk when mentally fatigued, they come up with new ideas: the physical act of walking probably acts as a mental stimulus.

We take the act of walking for granted, but it is

not an activity that comes naturally to all human beings. This is made evident by the story of the "wolf girls" Amala and Kamala. A baby would never stop crawling if he were surrounded by people who did nothing but crawl on hands and knees. That is why it is all the more important that a child be taught from the beginning to walk correctly.

There is a curious theory that a person who drags his feet has been made in infancy to wear shoes too large for his feet: he was forced to drag his feet in order to keep the shoes on. Whether or not this theory is true, it may well be possible to tell something about a person's level of intellect from the way he walks.

Motor Development Too Depends on Training

Keiko Ikeda's name is familiar to sports enthusiasts all over the world. She is the woman who distinguished herself in the gymnastics event at the Tokyo Olympics. In *Early Development,* I found the following article about Mrs. Ikeda.

Mr. and Mrs. Ikeda are both gymnasts. When their first baby was born, they devoted a great deal of attention to teaching him the Association's "baby exercises," and soon he could do somersaults. By the time he was in the second grade, he was able to jump from a chair, turning a somersault, and showing amazing promise in gymnastics. Pleased and content, Mr. and Mrs. Ikeda concluded that he had inherited their own abilities. Hence, assuming the talent was "in the blood," they did not give any training to their second child. This child, though born of the same athletic parents, could not do any gymnastic exercises, much less a somersault. By the example of their second child, Mr. and Mrs. Ikeda were made very much aware that motor ability has little to do with heredity.

It is true that one's physique and coordination are influenced by heredity, but how one uses what one is born with depends entirely on the training after birth. Even though one may be born with a physique suited for swimming, gymnastics, or other sports, without proper training such potential abilities will not actually be developed. In other words, a child born with an *inferior* physique could, with proper training in infancy, be developed to have superior abilities.

The "genius" brother and sister I've referred to who speak five languages were not particularly well built at birth. However, trained in jogging and push-ups in infancy, they grew up to be above average in their motor skills. The younger sister started to be trained by the father as early as eleven months, compared with her older brother, whose training began when he was two and a half. Because of this difference, though both are fast runners, the brother is not always the winner of his sports events, while the sister always comes in first without difficulty, even to waving her hand casually at the onlookers as she passes the post. Though they were born of the same parents, it was the difference in their ages when training started that caused this difference in their motor abilities.

This example illustrates once more how one's motor development depends on training after birth, rather than on one's genes. The so-called "inborn" athletic talent is really a matter of being "born into an athletic environment."

The Earlier One Takes Up a Sport, the Greater Facility One Will Develop

I have already said that an infant only a few months old can swim, and that a baby just learning to walk can roller-skate. On the other hand, an adult who can neither swim nor roller-skate will find it difficult to learn these skills: in fact, he may be so slow to acquire them that he gives up in despair.

These examples suggest that the motor responses should be trained while the brain is still like a piece of blank paper, before its circuit process is completed. I started golf in my late forties, but despite fifteen years' experience, I am still not a good player, and I feel somewhat discouraged. Had I started much earlier, I would have been far better than I am now without so much struggle.

An American acquaintance is very fond of golf. He had his two children learn to play golf early, the older son at the age of nine and the younger at the age of seven. Now, eight years later, the elder son's handicap is nine, but the younger son's is seven and he is by far the better player.

This does not necessarily mean that the younger son's motor responses are better developed than those of the older son. On the contrary, the latter is better built than the former and surpasses him in other sports. The father observed his children very closely to find out why the second son excels in golf, because he felt that the unraveling of this puzzle would be a key to more skillful golf-playing. However, he has not been able to find an answer to the mystery, the only clue that has come to mind being the fact that whereas the older son started golf at nine years of age, the younger began at seven. It seems that there is only one conclusion: the sooner one takes up a sport, the greater facility one can develop.

The Small Child Makes No Distinction Between Play and Work

I would like to give the following advice: "Let your small child do as much work as possible on condition that you do not expect results or completion."

In other words, to the young child, who makes no distinction between play and work, everything is play or everything is work. However extreme this may sound to the adult, it is very natural to the child.

To the small child every activity is purposeless— or rather, if there is any purpose, it lies in the doing itself. However, we adults have a notion that even a very simple task must be completed, and this notion makes us differentiate work from play. No matter how simple the job may be, we must teach the child how to do it, how to manipulate his fingers and use his body.

And work sometimes requires caution and concentration of mind which are not needed in play. A simple training in work, however, accelerates the development of the child's intellect and motor responses, and is worth the effort involved in teaching.

Dr. Seiji Kaya, former president of the University of Tokyo, remembers being asked many a time in his boyhood to weed the garden. Surprisingly, many parents seem to forget to take advantage, as a means of training the child, of such jobs as weeding, mopping, and watering, which are all closely related to daily life, and easy to teach. They are more concerned with music lessons, which are often beyond their capacity to teach.

It would indeed be easier for the parents to let their children play alone by themselves, for playing does not require teaching. It is a considerable effort to try to teach children to do jobs which they cannot be expected to do properly. But if parents, to spare themselves this trouble, rationalize by saying "It is cruel to make a child work," I think they are cheating their children.

Part V

SOME THINGS TO AVOID AND A GLANCE AT THE FUTURE

**Early Development Is Not a Preparatory Education
for Kindergarten and Primary School**

Since I started writing regularly in a weekly magazine about early development, I have received a variety of reactions, and many parents have written ac-
counts of their own experiences that have confirmed
my thoughts about early development.

There are, of course, doubters and opponents of
my ideas, but all in all parents show themselves enthusiastic about early development, though many of
them, unfortunately, still look upon early development as education for the talented or for producing
geniuses. One mother, who clearly grasps the concept
of the infinite potential in the child, seems to me
nevertheless to be seeing early development too literally in terms of preparation for school.

"Isn't there something wrong with the present
school education," she writes, "rather than with infant education? It is doubtful whether the present
education system is fit to further develop the abilities
that have been nurtured by early development. You
people speak of early development and such things,
but isn't it like withering a bud if the only purpose
the child is given at school is to score highest on
examinations?"

No parent is free of doubt about the present school

system, and I too have doubts. Every child follows the same path, entering elementary school at six years of age, then moving on to junior and senior high schools, and finally perhaps to a college or university. This system is very unsatisfactory to those who are talented and a heavy burden to those who are not so capable. A standard educational system cannot possibly produce men and women capable of assuming the responsibilities of the twenty-first century.

It is *because* of this very defect in the present educational system that I feel all the more acutely the necessity for early development. A child who has been trained properly in early development seems to do well in school. He seems to grow up at ease and in good health, in spite of the grade-getting system in schools. As long as a good bud has been implanted in the child in the most critical early years, he will grow up to be a strong child capable of surmounting any trying circumstances.

Furthermore, I cannot believe that the present educational system will last indefinitely. I trust in parents to insist on the changes that must come—with parents rests the destiny of our society and of future generations.

Neither Money Nor Time Is Needed for Early Development

I often receive the following objection to my theories: "I understand you very well, but I have neither money nor time to do so much for my child. Early development is, after all, only for a few people who have both money and time." However, being able to educate one's child is something different from being able to afford leisure or recreational activities. Educating a child is not so simple that it can be done only with time and money.

Among the parents whom I see sending their children for music lessons or instruction in a foreign language, there are indeed some who are doing it just to kill time or for the sake of their vanity. Decked out in expensive clothes and driving luxurious automobiles, they take their children to lessons just to show themselves off; it is no wonder that many regard early development as a pastime for the rich! But these are superficial aspects, and many poorer parents have to make a great effort to find time and money for lessons for their children.

However, lessons in music or in a foreign language are not the only means of developing your young child's potential. Any parents who are seriously concerned about their children will think of other educational ideas to replace music and language teaching. With this in mind, I have been thinking about alternatives, to the best of my ability.

If we assume that time and money are essential to the development of potential in the child, why is it that so many people born in rich homes turn out to have inferior abilities, and so many born in poor homes, great talents?

Surely education depends not on money and time, but on parental love and effort?

Parents Without Vision for the Future Are Incapable of Educating Their Children

Under the present educational system, almost everybody who studies can get into some college or university, regardless of his lineage, social standing, or financial means. This in itself is a wonderful fact, but, on the other hand, it has given rise to an evil: college education has become a be-all and end-all, and an unreal value has been set on academic careers.

In Japan and other countries, success in life is thought to be impossible without a college degree; hence, everybody studies. A degree from a first-class university guarantees a place in a prestigious company. So everybody pursues the same path, taking examination after examination right from kindergarten and elementary-school days. Hence, many parents look upon early development as one more way to give their children an early start, an early initiation into the exam-oriented system.

But how long will these current values last in this changing world? What is considered to be the most desirable now will not necessarily be so tomorrow, much less twenty to thirty years from now, when today's children are adults.

Your child will be of no use to the next generation if you bring him up with only the present in mind. For today's children will have to bear the responsibility of the twenty-first century, a century that is only twenty-odd years away but whose demands are beyond our imagination.

Parents who do not themselves have vision for the future cannot bring up children capable of assuming such responsibility. A shortsighted view of the present alone is not enough. There is no parent who does not wish and pray for the best for his or her child, but the most important thing is what the parent considers to be "fine" and "good." I do not think that parents who are so shortsighted as to evaluate only the present, and have no vision for the twenty-first century, can properly educate their children.

Nothing Is More Important than Child-Rearing

"I am too busy looking after my child to educate him as well. Ideal theories are all very well, but I can't possibly put them into practice."

I often meet with a response like this when I discuss my theories of early development. It seems to me, however, that making a distinction between child-rearing and child education is in itself the main mistake. Everyday rearing of children *is* infant education—that is, early development. The parent's attitude toward and feeling for the young child are what most subtly influence the child's development.

There are indeed mothers who feel they must go out to work for financial reasons, and also mothers who feel they are doing all they can by feeding the child and tending to his physical needs. But is there any education in the world better than a mother's affection?

Dr. Shinichi Suzuki speaks for me when he stresses the importance of mothering and mothers in the great enterprise of child-rearing. He has in fact been known to lecture parents very sternly about it.

"What do you mean, you cannot take care of your baby because you are too busy with other things? Is there any job in the world that is more important than rearing your baby? If there is, why did you have a baby?"

Parent Education Precedes Early Development

I have talked about the necessity of parents' changing their attitudes toward early development before it can be practiced rightly. Early development begins precisely with parent education. And everything I have written up to this point is a part of the education of the parents, in the sense that it has all been said to open their eyes to early development.

This way of speaking may seem a little insulting to the parents reading this book. But you cannot rely on another person to educate your child, particularly your infant. There is but one way: you the parent, particularly the mother, must strive to do it yourself by struggling to think and learn for yourself. There is no point in telling your young child, "This kind of education is good for you," or "You need this education." Your child cannot commit himself to the way in which he is reared because he has no choice.

Nor can you force your ideas on somebody else saying, "This is a good method of education; will you try it on my child and educate him?" Isn't it only right that parents should want to choose and decide for themselves, for the sake of their own children, on the educational theories and methods that are most convincing to them?

So the first thing, please, is to endeavor to educate yourself. Fortunately, the adult, unlike the small child, has a choice. But by this, I do not mean that the parents need to be educated in the academic sense of the word; I mean that they must try to learn voluntarily for themselves.

Those who go into teaching learn not only about their own disciplines—the subjects they teach—but also all the essentials of developmental psychology, and of the social and emotional processes by which we "become" human beings. Likewise, I wish that the mother, the first and greatest teacher of her infant, would learn for herself the basics of educational theory so that she can become really skilled in child-rearing.

The Parent Should Never Forget to Learn from the Child

One of the most dangerous traps into which the mother can fall in the bringing up of her child is that of complacency, which can be traced to her very enthusiasm. Meaning well for her child, she can unwittingly take on the role of an oppressor by imposing her own will on him.

This tendency is reinforced by the sheltered life that a mother often leads while involved in looking after house and children. She should not be made to feel that she alone is responsible for rearing her child, carrying the load entirely on her shoulders. She should have full support from the child's father and, if possible, also the grandfather and grandmother; and at the same time she should turn her attention to events in the world outside.

But most important of all, the mother should never forget to learn from her own child, so as not to fall into a habit of treating him in an authoritarian manner, according to her own concepts and her own needs.

William Wordsworth once wrote that "the child is father of the man," while Madame Montessori said that "the child is teacher of the man." These words were written not with special reference to early development. They are comments on the whole of life; the "man" has a great deal to learn from the "child."

Man has been aware of the importance of knowing his own self ever since the beginning of history, and has been striving toward that goal. His study of himself has involved theories backed up by science, by studies in biology, medicine, and psychology. And Madame Montessori makes the fascinating comment that whereas the first study of the human body was made on a corpse in an autopsy, the study of the human mind has been done with a newborn man, the infant.

I do not, of course, mean that you should undertake an academic course in the biological sciences or in philosophy. All I mean is that a mother who becomes complacent and dogmatic is likely to lose her own self; she becomes incapable of detached and calm observation and evaluation of her own thinking and attitudes. In order to avoid this, it is very important for the mother to be able to observe her young child objectively—what he says and feels, and how he behaves. In this approach to her child, what she finds will be a discovery of her own self and also of a knowledge that she can apply directly to the upbringing of her child.

The Sense in Which the Mother, Rather Than the Father, Helps the Child to Be a Fine Human Being

There have been many men in the world who have been called "geniuses." These are indeed extraordinarily talented individuals, many of whom have contributed a great deal to material progress and to the happiness of mankind. However, there is often another side to these men: many have not necessarily been happy in their own lives, because they were emotionally unstable or physically weak.

These men were not born geniuses, or born failures, or born weak. A study of their lives frequently reveals that the causes of their unhappiness go back to their early years and to the kind of education they received then. Their parents—their fathers in particular—were learned and ardent educators. There is nothing wrong in fathers' being learned and enthusiastic educators: on the contrary, it can be said that it was because of these fathers that their special talents were enabled to develop. However, these passionate educators did not allow their children to play with other children, and deprived of social contact and physical training, these children tended to grow up to be unbalanced human beings, however talented.

A good example is the French philosopher Blaise Pascal, author of the *Pensées.* Pascal was rigorously educated at home by his father, who, placing his hopes on his son in the years to come, retired from his position in the government in order to dedicate his life to the training of his child. The father taught his son geography, history, philosophy, languages, and mathematics. He did not cram the child with facts, but attempted with caution and consistency to inculcate in him an ability to think for himself. Pascal came to distinguish himself brilliantly later in life as a mathematician, physicist, and religious philosopher, and today there are few who are not familiar with the *Pensées,* or "Thoughts," in one form or another. The famous line "Man is only a reed, the weakest in nature, but he is a thinking reed" is Pascal's.

Yet most of the world does not know of this great man's confession that he did not have a single peaceful day after the age of eighteen in his short life of thirty-nine years. His mother died when he was three; hence, he had no recollection of his mother's affection. Deprived furthermore of association with other children, he knew only his father and his severe training. Is it not reasonable that such conditions would affect Pascal's physical constitution and mental makeup?

An abnormal genius may be reared by a father; but a human being well balanced in both mind and body needs the nurturing that traditionally comes from the mother. That is why I keep insisting on mothering as essential to early development.

Mothers Should Not Force Their Children in Early Development

The word "education" has for many come to connote coercion and pressure. That is why they misunderstand, and think that early development forces young children to do what they do not want to do, while ignoring their interests and desires. Of course, newborn babies cannot express clearly their likes and dislikes; however, the mother ought to be able to tell from her baby's responses what he is willing to accept and what he is not.

One of the mother's roles is to observe carefully what her baby wants, giving him the stimulation he craves. Forcing on the child what he does not want or coercing him to do what he has already lost interest in will produce nothing but frustration in the child.

It may be that because "education" implies a sense of "giving," anybody placed in a position to teach pulls himself together for the role. I myself regard the best of education in the "giving" sense as achieved outside the process we call "education" altogether. No parent, for instance, thinks of himself as having *taught* his native language when his child begins to speak it. Yet the stimulation to learn must have come in some way from the parents, even if no one calls it "education."

The mother's speech, actions, and feelings are always being transmitted to her child, influencing the formation of his ability and character. In other words, the daily life that the two lead together is an education, though it does not go by that name. Teaching something to the child is only one of the means of education. It is not the whole.

According to Mr. Akira Tago, associate professor at the University of Chiba, who has been studying the early years of prominent men, no educational method is more effective than that which stimulates a child to be motivated naturally, in a noncompulsory manner. It is the only right method. In short, the deep understanding and thoughtfulness of the mother and of those who surround the child is the very beginning of early development.

I have heard that F. W. Ostwald, the German chemist and author of *Great Men,* has a theory that geniuses are nurtured by suggestions and books. To these men, books were not something forced on them by their parents, but simply things always within reach of their hands. What they heard from their parents was not "You must become a great man," but rather the suggestion "I am sure you are capable of greatness."

172 SOME THINGS TO AVOID

Avoid the Abortion of Infant Education

Every year millions of babies come into this world.
In the past, families with five or six children were
not rare, as it was then said, "Go forth and multiply."
Nowadays, the average family has two children. In
other words, most of these babies have been planned
by their parents; they are the ones selected to be born
by parents who expect to be able to decide how many
children they will have. In this sense, they are privileged babies.

However, are these chosen babies being given an
education and an environment fit for the privileged?
I am afraid not. Though parents plan for the arrival
of a baby very carefully, once the baby is born they
tend to leave him to grow up in his own way. Yet it
hardly needs saying that it is more important to plan
carefully for the first three years of life than for the
period before birth.

There are many women in the world who have
abortions for no very serious reason. The world looks
upon abortion as evil; a burying alive of the seed of
life. On the other hand, however, the world is amazingly uncritical of parents who leave their children
unattended and uncared for after bringing them into
the world. Hiroshi Manabe calls these cases of neglect "the abortion of infant education." I too consider
this far more criminal than "abortion" itself.

There is no excuse for "abortion of infant education." It will bring unhappiness to homes and to the
world twenty to thirty years from now.

It is my suggestion that much of the strife and discontent among the youth in America today can be
put down to the "abortion of infant education" practiced by the American parents of twenty to thirty
years ago.

After the war, life in Japan, as in many countries, was a struggle for everybody, and children were inevitably left alone, uncared for and unattended. However, there is no longer any excuse for abortion in infant education.

Infants Are Not Their Parents' Possessions

A growing child reaches a point at which he is likely to talk back to his parents, saying, "I didn't ask to be born. So please don't be so nasty to me." How right he is! He is not here of his own will. The fact of his being here was entirely his parents' decision; they, therefore, are completely responsible for his upbringing until he grows up to be independent and self-sufficient.

However, it is amazing how many parents are under the illusion that they can do what they want with their children as long as the latter are their responsibility. They say, "I want to make my child an engineer," or "I wish to make my child a musician," seeking another's advice as thoughtlessly as if ordering a tailor to make a suit in a certain cut or style. Dr. Shinichi Suzuki often refers to mothers who, having decided to have their children take lessons in violin, ask him, "Dr. Suzuki, is my child going to amount to something?" He says he always replies, "No, he won't amount to *anything.*" The mother is, of course, very much shocked at first by this answer; but when she shows her disappointment, he adds the following remark: "Your child won't be *something,* but he will be a fine human being."

The maternal possessiveness reflected in this story is amazingly widespread. And it is this assumption that one's child is one's possession that is precisely what makes one ignore the child's own will. In fact, if a child is subjected to such treatment before he has yet developed his own will, he may find himself confused for life about who he really is. Instead of thinking of what one will *make* of one's child, one should focus on what one's child will *be.* The parent's duty is to give the child as many choices as possible so that he will be able to discover and decide for himself what he will be. For the child's future belongs neither to the parents nor to anybody else, but to the child himself.

A Mother's Lack of Confidence Is Harmful

At no other time in history has education been so universally thought of as leading to college education, nor have parents been so seriously concerned about the kind of education their children are receiving.

Unfortunately, the more anxious parents are about education, the more likely they are to lose their independence of thought, and to go for anything new just because it is new. Once previous educational methods were rejected, they jumped to the conclusion that everything in that system was wrong.

Such parents change from one fashion in education to another as easily as they change styles in clothing. Although it is said that there is now a boom in infant education, this is not so much because mothers understand the importance of early development as because they think it is the thing to do since everybody else is doing it.

There is nothing wrong with trying whatever one thinks is good; but the mother who wants to be the best teacher to her child cannot be so if she loses her own independence of thought. Both spartan education and the "let-alone" policy might be used as means to educate the child in different phases of growth and in different environmental conditions.

Shouldn't mothers be more confident in their approaches to their children? Trying one fashion after another will have only vitiating effects on the children. No matter how trivial the matter may be, the mother should try it on her child only after thorough consideration. Confidence and firmness in the mother are essentials in early development.

However, it is no good to the child if the mother is enslaved to wrong ideas and never makes any concessions. Nor will it help him if she approaches her task in too casual or happy-go-lucky a way. Educating the child is the greatest task the mother has, and there is no labor-saving shortcut in this job. I want mothers to develop their own way of thinking about early development by freeing themselves from fashionable fixed or easygoing approaches.

Vanity in the Mother Implants False Values in a Child

"My child is very special, so I am going to let him take piano lessons." "Our neighbor's child is taking violin lessons, so my child shall do the same."

Such attitudes are still found in many mothers who are motivated solely by their vanity.

It is not an exaggeration to say that this sort of attitude is partially responsible for the unfair prejudice against early development as education for the elite, or for genius. In fact, the children induced by snobbish mothers to take violin lessons are somewhat lacking in innocence and are often cheeky, as though their mothers had implanted in them the false values of prestige and competitiveness. The violin and piano lessons, meant to develop the potential in children, are actually gnawing at their hearts.

There is nothing special about piano lessons or the ability to play the piano, which is nothing but a means to an end. The focus should be placed on what the child gets out of it and what ability he develops through it. There is nothing particularly grand or magnificent about piano and violin lessons in themselves, as these supercilious mothers think.

For instance, in Dr. Suzuki's violin class there are always many children who are better players than others. There is no possibility that some one child can come to think that he alone plays the violin well. So the ambition of the mother who wants her child alone to excel cannot possibly be gratified—either she will have to throw off her false pride or her child will have to stop taking lessons.

Of course, pride in one's skill in violin playing is another thing altogether, and is something that can help the child to grow. My own son has gained great self-confidence through violin lessons, and consequently has improved in other fields as well.

In Order to Improve Your Child, You as Parent Must First Change and Improve Yourself

"He does not understand how his parents feel," complains many a parent when a child is disobedient. Is it really true that the children are in the wrong? I myself think that the parents are to blame.

Dr. Suzuki told me of a certain mother who had not been able to get along well with her child: a great deal of hostility had been generated between them. The mother, in distress, used to say, "What a terrible child I have been given. It must be my bad luck." But Dr. Suzuki told her, "It's all because of your treatment of your child. You scold him too much to make him behave, and your child is always on his guard and is bound to wear a sour expression. There should be respect even in the relationship between parent and child. Don't you think your child will understand and respect you better if you admit to him that you can be wrong too?" Some time after that, the mother, looking pleased, came to see Dr. Suzuki and told him that after her talk with him she had dealt with her child in a more humble way and he had softened. Thus she regained communication and rapport with him.

So-called "education-mamas" often complain that whenever they are a little demanding of their children, the latter, if they are sensitive at all, become discontented and say, "You, Mother, can say what you like, because you don't have to do it yourself." The children are right, and the mothers cannot say a word to refute them. Telling children to do this and that will not get parents anywhere: they must first do it themselves and have the children learn afterward. If the children are exerting themselves to the limit, and their parents are doing only one-tenth or one-half of their share, that will not do. I do not mean that parents should make efforts in the same way in everything that the children must do; but there must be a way of showing your efforts as parents.

Mr. Manabe says that he perspires all over when

he takes a bath with his children (Japanese baths are big enough for two persons). He does not mean that he has to compete with his children to see who can stay in the steaming bathroom longer: he means that in order to keep his children in the bathtub, he has to tell them some sort of story. But if the story is the same every day they will not be content, so he has to struggle desperately to think up new stories. "If you are good, I'll buy you something" will not get him anywhere. So he racks his brain to create new stories or stretch out old ones, as in *The Arabian Nights*.

Ordering the child "Do this," or "Memorize this," while the father sits back comfortably, doing nothing and thinking, "Oh, when this little creature gets to be a big man, I too will get some benefit," is a lazy way of bringing up a child. And certainly no one will succeed in early development with his own child unless he is prepared to make as much effort as Mr. Manabe. Bringing up children means bringing up and developing oneself, first of all.

Rearing the Child to Excel the Parent Is True Education

There is an old saying, "Deeper is the blue extracted from the indigo plant." The blue dye extracted from the indigo plant is indeed of a deeper color than the plant itself, and the meaning of the proverb is "It is a case of a disciple's outshining his master." This, I believe, should be the fundamental goal of education.

I have said from time to time that ability is not

inborn. And even if we should accept the theory that ability is one hundred percent inborn, the child should still grow up at least to reach the level of his parents. Therefore, if the parents cannot bring up their child to excel them even by a little, it can be because of nothing but their own laziness, as the parents are the first and greatest teachers of the child.

In *My Theory of Early Development,* Dr. Suzuki tells of an interesting experience. Here it is:

In our Talent Education School, we have the children listen many times to a recording of the violin music they are practicing. Then I say to them, "Please play a little better than the record." The pupils, being little children, say, "Yes" and proceed to play it, trying to excel the record. Very soon they do play a little better than the record. It is not very difficult to excel the record, for it is a recording of my own playing.

Generally speaking, the fundamental idea of our school is to train children to be better than their teachers. We call the children who excel me "student" and those who don't "apprentice student." We would end up regressing to the Stone Age if the student, having failed to reach the standard of his teacher's playing, then himself became a teacher and were in turn unable to train his students to attain his own level. If this were to happen, we would not be able to hope for the advancement and progress of culture. The student is bound to excel his teacher.

Needless to say, there is no parent who does not wish to bring up his child to be superior to himself. Even in the academic field, there is absolutely no need to give in to the idea that one's child's capacities are limited because one's own happen to be so.

Men and Women Capable of Trusting Others Will Build the Twenty-first Century

Our present world is in a state of flux. Technological progress has made our lives amazingly rich and convenient. Twenty years ago electronic computers could merely count numbers a little faster than the human brain, but these have been improved to a point of performing nearly all the tasks the human brain can perform.

And there is no end to similar examples. Technological progress has brought about not only affluence and easy living, but changes in our thinking also. Once people have found material fulfillment, they begin to seek spiritual enrichment. People are now seriously thinking of the role of mankind in life as well as the meaning of what man ought to be. However, it is not easy to change oneself once one is already grown up, just because the world around us changes. Therefore, the new society of the future can be entrusted only to the young children who are now growing up. This has been the reason for my attaching so much importance to early development.

A mere look at the world is enough to confirm the lack of trust among people. Chaos in society, pollution, and violence all have their cause in lack of mutual trust. However convenient and affluent our lives may be, we cannot possibly live in peace and happiness in a society that is lacking in trust.

Anybody older than preschool age can understand

what it means to trust people and not to cause trouble for others. However, understanding principles and yet not being able to put them into practice is the nature of man. No feeling of trust is nurtured among people if they simply practice principles because they have been taught them and they seem reasonable. Only knowing these principles innately and learning them naturally will enable man for the first time to trust his fellows. If the pattern of these principles is implanted in the child in his earliest years, he will be sure to grow up wonderfully capable of assuming the responsibility of a future society.

Even if a child is a little more intelligent and clever than other children, yet is without the feeling of trust, he will not amount to much in the future.

Because the present educational system emphasizes the importance of examinations and grades, it ignores and discourages instilling trust in man. That is why it is all the more important to implant a firm basis of trust in a child before kindergarten and school age, so that he may grow up to trust others. That is the true objective of early development.

Today's Young Children Alone Will Be Capable of Eradicating Wars and Racial Prejudices

I have repeatedly stated that my thinking about early development does not originate in any idea of producing specialists and geniuses, but rather in my hopes of educating every infant to develop fully his potential abilities and to grow up courageous in thought and straightforward in character.

While we sing the praises of our high level of civilization and the expansion of our economy, we still witness on this earth wars, racial prejudice, and hostilities among nations, in spite of the fact that people all over the world have been reaching out for promotion of world peace through such organizations as the United Nations, UNESCO, and WHO. However, it is almost an impossible task for our generation to create a peaceful world where people can sincerely trust and tolerate one another. Hatred inherited for generations, hostility between the ruler and the ruled, antagonism and suspicion have come to seem almost biological in their nature—at least for countries other than one's own—and once one has been imbued with these feelings, one cannot easily be freed from them.

We adults must not instill these prejudices and misunderstandings in the infants who are to assume the responsibility of the future. Children below the age of three have no ideas of racial prejudice and hatred for other races. If in this period children of different races were brought up *equally* together, they would grow up accepting quite naturally that there are all sorts of people, of different colors, just as there are different faces and tall and short people. However, if they should grow up imbued with prejudices, it could only be the fault of adults injecting their own feelings. It may be that if one seriously hopes for world peace, one should be deeply concerned about the world's present political situations—but is it not *more* urgent to give one's attention to the education of the infant who will be the pillar of future society, and to be willing to devote oneself to this task, even if the cost is high? True world peace no longer depends on us, the adults of the present, but on the generation who are at present infants.

I do not consider my hopes for the infants inordinate. I have absolutely no idea how effective my views and activities will be toward the realization of such hopes. I also do not consider that what I have been putting forward in this book is not open to criticism, including my fundamental ideas, my detailed explanation of various methods, and my estimates of the mother's role. However, I do hope that this book will create a change in the world, in activating people's interest in early development, particularly in the education of children below the age of three. Toward this goal, I firmly believe this book will serve as the first step.